Reclaiming Catholic Social Teaching

Also by Anthony Esolen
from Sophia Institute Press:

Reflections on the Christian Life:
How Our Story Is God's Story

Anthony Esolen

Reclaiming Catholic Social Teaching

A Defense of the Church's True Teachings on Marriage, Family, and the State

SOPHIA INSTITUTE PRESS
Manchester, New Hampshire

Sophia Institute Press
Box 5284, Manchester, NH 03108
1-800-888-9344

www.SophiaInstitute.com

Sophia Institute Press® is a registered trademark of Sophia Institute.

Library of Congress Cataloging-in-Publication Data

Esolen, Anthony M.
    Reclaiming Catholic social teaching : a defense of the Church's true teachings on marriage, family, and the state / Anthony Esolen.
        pages cm
    Includes bibliographical references.
    ISBN 978-1-62282-182-2 (pbk. : alk. paper) 1. Christian sociology—Catholic Church. 2. Leo XIII, Pope, 1810-1903. 3. Catholic Church—Doctrines. I. Title.
    BX1753.E69 2014
    261.8088'282—dc23

                                                        2014020772

First printing

This book is dedicated to my grandparents: John and Mary Esolen and Peter and Angeline Conserette. They came from Italy without any money, but with a will to work hard and to raise strong and virtuous children. They lived in material poverty, but they possessed the natural moral virtues of temperance, wisdom, justice, and the one without which the others are but words—courage. They held the ramparts for their families against despair and the follies of the day. All that I owe to my parents I also owe to them; and may God let perpetual light shine upon them.

Contents

Abbreviations

Full bibliographical details and other works cited are listed at the end of the book. Numbers in the references throughout the text refer to the page numbers of the translation from which the quotation was taken.

AP	*Aeterni Patris*	LE	*Les Evenements*
AD	*Arcanum divinae*	LP	*Libertas*
AMC	*Au Milieu des consolations*		*praestantissimum*
		LO	*Longinquae oceani*
AMS	*Au Milieu des solicitudes*	MC	*Mirae caritatis*
		ME	*Militantis Ecclesiae*
AV	*Affari vos*	PAA	*Pervenuti all'anno*
CMS	*Cum multa sint*	PD	*Providentissimus Deus*
D	*Diuturnum*	QAM	*Quod Apostolici muneris*
EIA	*Exeunte iam anno*		
GDC	*Graves de communi*	RN	*Rerum novarum*
HG	*Humanum genus*	SC	*Sapientiae Christianae*
ID	*Immortale Dei*	T	*Tametsi*
I	*Inscrutabili*	TB	*Testem benevolentiae*

Reclaiming Catholic Social Teaching

A Return to First Principles

*It shall even be as when an hungry man dreameth,
and, behold, he eateth, but he awaketh, and his soul
is empty: or as when a thirsty man dreameth, and,
behold, he drinketh; but he awaketh, and behold, he is
faint, and his soul hath appetite: so shall the multitude
of all the nations be, that fight against mount Zion.*
—Isaiah 29:8

*Wherefore do ye spend money for that which is not
bread? And your labor for that which satisfieth not?
Hearken diligently unto me, and eat ye that which
is good, and let your soul delight itself in fatness.*
—Isaiah 55:2

I s it possible, I have sometimes wondered, for a well-intended and intelligent person to get everything wrong, in the very matter upon which he sets his mind most energetically?

It is more than possible. If he begins from false principles, and if he is relentlessly logical, and if he looks askance at common sense, at traditions that are the distilled wisdom of many generations and at the evidence of human affairs around him, he not only may get everything wrong; he *must* get everything wrong.

If he were less logical, or more easily distracted from his ideas by the stubborn realities around him, he might blunder back into truth once in a while. But if he clings to the false principles, if they become to him a ruling deity, then he will be like Chesterton's madman who has lost everything *but* his reason. Or he will be like a carpenter whose tools are out of kilter. His T-square is oblique, his straightedge is crooked, his level wobbles, his plumb line drifts. If he keeps on building with those tools, never stepping back to look at what he has actually wrought, he will not have built a bad house; he will not have built a house at all. He will have built a wreck, a monstrosity. The first strong wind will send it toppling.

Even if his tools are right, if he refuses to respect the *nature* of the materials he builds with, he will succeed only in building a great ruin. Maybe, in some world of his dreams, willow *should* be as strong as oak, marble *should* be as light as concrete, and sand *should* be as stable as rock. But we must build in this world that we live in. In this world, a carpenter of long experience can tell you how to work with beams that are never going to be exactly straight. In this world, a mason of long experience can tell you how to build with stones that are never quite identical in shape and size. In the world of somebody's logical dreams, a boy with half the strength of a man may cut down an oak tree in twice the time. In this world, the ax will break the boy and leave his hands covered with blisters before he gets anywhere near the heart of the tree.

As in carpentry and masonry, so in human affairs. We must have good tools, and we must respect the material we work with; that is, we must begin from correct principles, and we must be steeped in humanity. We must know what human beings are, what they are for—or, to put it a different way, what perfection they should seek. We must also know their limitations, physical, emotional, and intellectual. And we must be honest about their moral weakness, what Christians call their fallen nature. Because any one person's experience is going to be quite limited, we must avail ourselves of the long experience of mankind that is summed up in that sad and glorious thing called history. Add to all of this that "we" the builders are also the objects of the building. We must be honest about ourselves.

The person who seeks out first principles, and who at the same time fixes his gaze upon human realities, is not likely to be fooled by phantasms. He is not likely to mistake a dream of bread for the real thing. Imagine someone appealing to Lord Baden-Powell, founder of the Boy Scouts, to justify the activities of gangs in Los Angeles. Baden-Powell wanted boys to do risky things, and what's more dangerous than running guns or smuggling cocaine or fighting another gang in a shooting spree?

A Return to First Principles

He enjoined upon the Scouts a stern code of honor and loyalty, and who is more loyal than a recruit for the Crips? Who is more willing to shed his blood for the honor of the gang?

The reply must be, "You are mistaking a phantasm for a reality. That is because you have not gotten back to principles, and you are not really looking closely at human nature. It is not mere *risk* that we promote, but valor, staking all that you are for something truly noble, something that might well earn you the ridicule of the street crowd. We know that boys are attracted to danger. We do not seek to change that, even if we could. We want them instead to be attracted to something far more adventurous than a street brawl. We know that we can do this, because it has been done before, and that is something you seem to have forgotten."

Or imagine someone appealing to Michelangelo to justify pornography. Michelangelo painted nudes all over the Sistine Chapel. He endured the disgruntlement of the prudish, so that the figures in his Last Judgment were later provided with discreet veils and tunics and loincloths. He admired the sculpture of ancient Greece, and there are pieces of Greek pottery that would make even a high school health teacher blush. So why should a busy stockbroker in a hotel not relax in front of a television, watching whatever delights his sophisticated tastes?

The reply must be, "You are mistaking a phantasm for a reality, even while you appear to yourself to be considering nothing but a material fact, that there are nudes in both cases. But a doctor with a scalpel is not the same thing as a thief with a scalpel. Michelangelo sought to exalt the beauty of the human form, even as he shows us our fall into sin and confusion. He sought to remind us of the glory that is still ours, though we have tarnished it and half forgotten it. That is not the case with the pornographer, whose work appeals only to the brutish or demonic within us, so that we do not actually care about the persons or the faces on the screen. Michelangelo lifts up and liberates. The other suppresses what is most human, and enslaves. You may say that it *need not* be so. You might as well say that men *need not* grow filthy by living among swine. But they *will*."

First principles and human realities — we must return to them. They are what this book is about.

Imagine someone appealing to Florence Nightingale to justify doctor-dosed suicide, on the grounds that she wanted to relieve suffering. Imagine someone appealing to St. Francis of Assisi to justify looting, on the grounds that his heart was with the poor. Imagine someone appealing to St. Catherine of Siena to justify a famous American feminist who says that human progress requires abortion on demand, on the grounds that Catherine was a strong woman who gave the Pope himself doses of bitter and salutary advice.

The phantasms of materialists, whose principles are wrong and who cannot even see the material reality before them!

Imagine a lawyer returning his fee when he loses a case; imagine a television pundit suddenly admitting that he doesn't know what he is talking about; imagine a Hollywood starlet speaking English; imagine anything most absurd, and you have not yet approached the absurdity of those who claim that Catholic social teaching implies the existence of a vast welfare state, utterly secular, materialist in all its assumptions about a good life, bureaucratically organized, unanswerable to the people, undermining families, rewarding lust and sloth and envy, acknowledging no virtue, providing no personal care, punishing women who take care of their children at home, whisking the same children into vice-ridden schools designed to separate them from their parents' views of the world, and, for all that, keeping whole segments of the population mired in generations of dysfunction, moral squalor, and poverty, while purchasing their votes with money extorted from their neighbors.

It is manifestly absurd to suppose that Catholic teaching regarding sex and marriage is one thing, in an old-fashioned trinket box, while Catholic teaching regarding stewardship and our duties to the poor is another thing, on a marble pedestal. It is absurd to suppose that Catholic teaching regarding the Church and her authority is one thing, the Latinate red-edged tome tucked away in a closet, while Catholic teaching regarding the laity is another, marching in parade. No, it is all of a piece. What the Church says about divorce is inextricable from what she says about the poor. What she says about the presence of Christ in the Eucharist is inextricable from what she says about human dignity. When we fail to see the integrity of the Faith, not only do certain truths escape our notice; the rest, the truths we think we see, grow monstrous, like cancers, and destroy the flesh they once seemed to restore.

The reason should be obvious to all believers. We worship one God, the Lord of all. The Word of God is not one thing at one time, and another thing at another time: it is Christ, the same yesterday, today, and tomorrow (cf. Heb. 13:8). There is only one name by which we may be saved, says St. Peter (Acts 4:12). It is not possible to kneel to the Lord on Sunday, while giving the "secular" days to Mammon or Baal, or to a deified State going by the name of Ramses or Tiberius or the Republic or whatever may be the fashion of the time.

Jesus prayed that we might be one, even as He and the Father are one (John 17:11). Therefore, Catholics believe that the Lord established one Church upon earth, not a variety to meet the tastes and appetites of various men or various ages. I understand that the Church of Christ has been divided. Let it be considered as punishment for our sins, and never as something to be desired. To believe otherwise, to believe that there should be a church with one moral code for John, and another church with another code for Joseph, or a church to be endlessly tailored to fit the times, is essentially to deny the immutability and the unity of God. It is to worship ourselves instead.

The bonds of love that should unite man to God and neighbor to neighbor follow from the fact that man himself is one. Schizophrenia is no part of the original plan of the Creator. I cannot say I possess a religious self here that honors God in monetary matters, but a secular self there that reserves sexual matters to my all-determining will. Nor can I do the reverse. Jesus comes not to save parts of us—there are no such things. He comes to save indivisible souls. Sin vitiates not simply this or that faculty, but the whole man, since it is the whole man who sins, and the whole man who must be redeemed.

So if we are going to talk about the social teaching of the Church, we must address some fundamental questions: Who is God? What is man? How is man oriented toward God as the fount and aim of his being and his beatitude? Why has God made man a social being? What is a society? Why do we join with others? What is the first and foundational society? What is society for? What does virtue have to do with the good of man—man the social being? Is man capable of forming a just society without the aid of religion? Can that even make sense, granted who and what man is? How does sin vitiate man's reason, so that he mistakes appearances for reality? How does it vitiate man's will, so that he turns toward the evil that is near and easy, and not toward the good that is far and difficult? Can he attain the blessings even of this world, let alone the world to come, without grace? Can he, the social being, attain them while remaining outside of the special society ordained by God, the society that is a guide and a model for all other societies?

We must return to principles.

With that in mind, I turn to the writings of Pope Leo XIII.

Pope Leo is sometimes called the founder of Catholic social teaching. He would have been appalled by the credit. He intended nothing other than to apply to current concerns what Jesus taught His Apostles and what they handed down to their successors. He intended to teach nothing new. He is blessedly free of the mercurial ingenuity of a vain scholar and the meddlesome pride of an innovator. His thoughts derive not from the nature of the spanking-new modern State, nor from social advances sometimes more apparent than real, but from the changeless nature of man, discoverable by reason and frank observation, and by humble attention to the revealed word of God. Leo never supposed that one could devise any social teaching without understanding what a society is to begin with, which requires that we understand what human beings are, and *why they are* — for what end God made them, male and female, in His image and likeness. Leo surveys the world from a mountaintop. He possessed a manifestly keen mind, but it was not that mind that gave him the vantage. It was the Faith.

He also surveys the world from the lesser but still grand promontory of natural reason. He heeds what the greatest thinkers, including the pagan philosophers of Greece and Rome, have to teach us. He draws upon that vast fund of human experience that is called *history*. His principles are not his own, but his reasoning from those principles is exact and clear. His conclusions, granting the premises, are irresistible. His predictions regarding what would happen if the Church were shouldered from her rightful duties are more than prescient. That would imply a special gift of foresight that he nowhere claims. They are simply *inevitable*. They also have come to pass.

Let us then turn first to God.

1

Man, in the Image of God

One thing have I desired of the LORD, *that will I seek after: that I may dwell in the house of the* LORD *all the days of my life, to behold the beauty of the* LORD, *and to inquire in his temple.*
—Psalm 27:4

Yet man, this part of your creation, wishes to praise you. You arouse him to take joy in praising you, for you have made us for your-self, and our heart is restless until it rests in you.
St. Augustine, *Confessions*, 1.1

The most fundamental truth about man is that he has been made by God, who is Himself love. He is made by God, in the image of God, *for God*. He is made for the enjoyment of that fullness of being. Nothing short of that aim will suffice.

Should someone say, "That is all well and good, if that is what you believe, but we must construct our societies according to a secular understanding of man," we must reply that both of us cannot be correct. If the Catholic Christian view is correct, if man is made by God, in His image, for the enjoyment of the very life of God, then any society built upon other premises will be radically deficient. I mean more than that it will not be perfect. Nothing that man constructs will ever be perfect. I mean that it will be constructed according to false principles; as if you should attempt to build a barricade out of paper, or a canoe out of lead; or to feed a child with sand. It would mistake the nature of the being it purports to satisfy.

Aleksandr Solzhenitsyn once said that the simple truth about our time, the one thing that explains the emptiness of modern life in the materially wealthy West and the cruelties that he suffered in his own person in materialist Russia, was that man had forgotten God. It is one thing never to have known Him, says Pope Leo. That involves no ingratitude, but "after having known, to reject or forget Him, is such a horrible and mad crime as to be scarcely credible" (*Tametsi* [1900], 463). Like St. Augustine in his wayward youth, man seeks from mere matter what matter has not in itself to give. In the very constitution of his being, he longs for joy that can never be taken away, but sinks instead into the tedium and disappointment of pleasures, or the hectic excitement of wickedness.

Pope Leo saw the conflict between a full vision of man and its secular reduction. In *Rerum novarum*, his grand treatise on the condition of the working classes, he notes that if we truncate man, excluding from our purview the eternal end for which he was made, "the very notion of what is good and right would perish; nay, the whole scheme of the universe would become a dark and unfathomable mystery. The great truth which we learn from Nature herself is also the grand Christian dogma on which Religion rests as on its foundation—that when we have given up this present life, then shall we really begin to live" (220).

That can sound as if the Catholic must ignore the present life, so long as he is walking the way to salvation. But that would be to commit an error like that of the Naturalists, whom Pope Leo, in *Humanum genus* and other letters, consistently condemns. They sever the bond that joins nature to her Creator and strive so that "the office and authority of the Church may become of no account in the civil state; and for this reason they declare to the people and contend that Church and State ought to be altogether disunited" (*HG*, 90). I will be saying more about that relationship in the next chapter. For the moment, I'd like to note that Leo's language suggests that such a severance is *unnatural*: the self-styled Naturalists argue "rem sacramque civilem esse penitus distrahendas" ("that the sacred and the civil *thing* should be torn apart to the core"). But man is the subject of both. To tear them apart is to tear him apart. It is one thing to note that they are *different* things: heaven is not earth. It is quite another to argue that they are utterly distinct, having nothing to do with one another.

Again, this truth flows from the very being of the Creator. God has not simply made a thing and let it be. He is wholly and intimately present in every smallest measure of space, in every shortest blink of time. There is no life but from God. "God alone is Life," says Leo. "All other beings partake of, but are not, life.... From [Christ], as from its ultimate and most august beginning, all life has flowed down upon the world and will forever flow; all that is, has its being from Him; all that lives, lives by Him, for by the Word 'all things were made, and without Him was nothing made that was made'" (T, 473). That is why, as we will see, Pope Leo continually appeals to nature itself as giving witness to the glory of God, and as something whose integrity we must respect and whose laws we must obey. Grace does not supplant nature, but perfects it.

Therefore, to treat human nature as simply separate from God, and thus to attempt to construct a civil society without reference to God, is to treat of a thing that does not exist, and to attempt to build a society upon that fiction. Moreover, it is to rob civil society of the very thing that can bring it as close as possible to peace on earth. We are too apt to think that our troubles arise from the particularities of this or that law, as if a house falling apart might be shored up if we simply replaced one rotten rafter. Pope Leo looks at the foundation.

Who would suppose that false principles in philosophy, of all things, would lead to destruction in the State? Yet that is what Leo says, again and again. The error may go by various names, but the parentage is the same: the denial of the intimate relationship of the Creator with His creation. "Whoso turns his attention to the bitter strifes of these days," writes Leo in *Aeterni Patris*, his great treatise promoting the true naturalism of St. Thomas Aquinas, "and seeks a reason for the troubles that vex public and private life, must come to the conclusion that a fruitful cause of the evils which now afflict, as well as those which threaten us, lies in this: that false conclusions concerning divine and human things, which originated in the schools of philosophy, have crept into all the orders of the State, and have been accepted by the common consent of the masses" (35).

One of those false conclusions, to which we shall frequently return, is that human rights are granted by the State, or by the mere power of numbers. Americans remember the Declaration of Independence, wherein Thomas Jefferson, no friend to the Catholic Church, called our rights "inalienable." The word is apt to be misunderstood. It means more than that no one else has the right to take them from us. It means that *we do not even have the right to alienate them from ourselves.* It implies that we are *not the source of our rights*, because otherwise we could declare our own rights to be null, or "we," that is, the majority, or the State, could do so. The only reasonable source for rights that oblige us, *even if we do not want them*, is God. Even the poor workman, under pressure from unscrupulous employers, may not alienate these rights: "No man has in this matter power over himself. To consent to any treatment which is calculated to defeat the end and purpose of his being is beyond his right; he cannot give up his soul to servitude" (*RN*, 233).

So Pope Leo writes to the church in France. He desires, in *Au Milieu des solicitudes* (1892), both to recognize that the French republic is a legitimate form of government, to which all good Catholics owe their allegiance, and to affirm that God, not the people or the emperor, is the source of its authority. Only what transcends us and our many affairs here on earth, with all our conflicting interests, can unite us. This truth is both pragmatic (nothing else really works) and existential (we desire a harmony of *souls*, not simply an orderly management of bodies):

> Now morality, in man, by the mere fact that it should establish harmony among so many dissimilar rights and duties, since it enters as an element into every human act, necessarily supposes God, and with God, religion, that sacred bond whose privilege is to unite, anteriorly to all other bonds, man to God. Indeed, the idea of morality signifies, above all, an order of dependence in regard to truth which is the light of the mind; in regard to good which is the object of the will; and without truth and good there is no morality worthy of the name. And what is that principal and essential truth, that from which all truth is derived? It is God. What, therefore, is the supreme good from which all other good proceeds? God. Finally, who is the creator and guardian of our reason, our will, our whole being, as well as the end of our life? God; always God. (AMS, 251)

If this is *not true*, then, as Dostoyevsky famously put it, all things are permissible. I know there are atheists who believe we can build a morality up from odds and ends of old sentiments, political expedience, self-interest, and more or less popularly acknowledged "goods." In vain. Those things alone are no stronger than straw. What obliges me to accept another man's calculation of utility? You may say that a taste for brawling in the streets is obviously evil, because it upsets the good order that should prevail in suburbs flush with material comforts. But upsetting that order is precisely what I intend! What you call good order, I call dreariness. And I have Mikhail Bakunin and his fellow anarchists at my back. Nor am I impressed by your material comforts. Why should men be soft and pampered? What *obliges* me, in your moral system? Bare rationality? But I find it unreasonable to commit myself to so insipid and mechanical a life. The threat of force? Obey, or find yourself behind bars? Then your system amounts to no more than the will of numbers. A villain may resist the will of numbers. So may a hero.

But I will not labor the point. All people who believe in God must grant it. It is also ratified, Leo observes, by the history of all peoples: "Religion, and religion only, can create the social bond" (AMS, 250). By "religion" he does not mean an opinion that one may or may not harbor. Here the French of Leo's letter, and the Latin it is based upon, come to our assistance. The "social bond" is not a matter of mere feeling. It is *le lien social*: something that binds us, one to another, in sacred duty. That is the inner meaning of the Latin *religio*: a binding. Religion is not in the first instance a system of beliefs about God and man. It is the happy virtue of granting to God what is His due.

And since man is not a disembodied spirit, or a free-floating atom of self-will—since man is an embodied soul, made for love of God and neighbor—the duties of religion cannot remain notional, in the mind alone. "Religion," says Leo, "is the interior and exterior expression of the dependence which, in justice, we owe to God" (AMS, 251). What that implies is clear. All citizens, he says, bear the grave responsibility of binding themselves one to another (*s'allier*) to maintain in the nation "true religious sentiment, and to defend it in case of need, if ever, despite the protestations of nature and of history, an atheistical school should set about banishing God from society, thereby surely annihilating the moral sense even in the depths of the human conscience."

Man, in the Image of God

The Social Need for Religion

James Madison famously said that the Constitution of the United States had been drafted for a moral and religious people, and no other. He may stand at the head of a long line of social commentators who see that it is useful to have religion around, because without religion, liberty soon degenerates into license, and then the society goes to smash. But Pope Leo says much more than that. We must insist upon the difference. It is not a difference of degree or emphasis. It is a difference in kind.

What the Pope says to the Frenchmen of his day bears repeating now to all people who forget the highest aim of man:

> When different families, without giving up the rights and
> duties of domestic society, unite under the inspiration
> of nature, in order to constitute themselves members
> of another larger family circle called civil society, their
> object is not only to find therein the means of providing
> for their material welfare, but, above all, to draw thence
> the boon of moral improvement. (AMS, 250-51)

It is remarkable that those final words should strike us as remarkable. They would not have puzzled the greatest political philosopher the world has known, Aristotle. They would not have puzzled his greater disciple, St. Thomas Aquinas. They follow from a plain observation of man.

What distinguishes man from beast? We both need food and drink. Birds have their nests, and man builds his cottage. Mares must bear foals, women must bear children. Now, if the perfection of a creature involves the full development and best action of what distinguishes it from other creatures, what can that faculty be in man, if not the virtue of the reasoning mind? But the mind is not some disembodied thing.

The ancient Greeks sought *wisdom* and knew well that wisdom implied far more than the possession of a bundle of facts. An encyclopedia is not wise. Nor was Charles Dickens's notorious schoolmaster, Thomas Gradgrind. He taught only facts, facts, facts and therefore missed the human truth before him, the truth of his desperately sad family. The Greeks wanted to *see* (that is the inner meaning of our English word *wisdom*, as also of its Latin-derived cousin *vision* and its Greek-derived cousin *idea*) and to act accordingly. The wise man sees what is true and instructs his will to follow it. He falls in *love* with that truth, as Plato suggests in the *Phaedrus*. His virtue is therefore both contemplative and active.

So if human beings unite to help one another to attain the *good* that is most properly theirs, then we cannot say that they simply encourage morality or religion, so that the trains will run on time and their stores will be stocked with good food. It is the reverse. We want the material needs to be met, because they are real and important, but above all because their satisfaction will give us the leisure to meet the more important needs, which are moral and spiritual. We need one another not just so that one man will be a farmer and another man a carpenter. We need one another because our common life together provides for the exercise of moral virtue; and because the wisest and best among us will help us in our quest to attain that virtue. We depend upon one another for our *perfectionnement moral*: our moral growth toward perfection. We need one another, for love.

It is stunning to consider how thoroughly we wish we could deny the undeniable. We say, "Civil society demands that we not make any moral judgments," when in fact that would leave us in a wilderness of incivility. We would have to set aside what makes us human. Leo draws the obvious conclusion. Suppose we construct our civil "society" to satisfy material needs, but no others. Then, he says, "society would rise but little above the level of an aggregation of beings devoid of reason, and whose whole life would consist in the satisfaction of sensual instincts" (AMS, 251). From force of habit we might call such a thing a society, but it would really be a mere herd, a corral. Appetites and not wisdom would rule; and appetites go where the force of numbers leads. In that case, says Leo, we would be hard put to show "that civil society was an advantage rather than a detriment to man." Better to live in a wilderness of bears and bobcats, than in a dreadful jungle of beasts endowed with intelligence.

That jungle goes by another name. According to Augustine, the whole history of the human race is an everlasting battle between two cities, the City of Man and the City of God. That division provides the framework for the Pope's thoughts, in *Humanum genus* (1884), about man's attempts to build a society without God. For the one city "steadfastly contends for truth and virtue, the other for those things which are contrary to virtue and to truth" (HG, 83). For Leo, virtue and truth, what we might call the highest aims of the active life and of the contemplative life, are distinct but inseparable, as are man's will and his intellect. That intimacy is suggested by the Latin Leo uses: the true citizens, those of the City of God, contend for *veritate et virtute*: truth and manhood, truth and fidelity to the truth. The mock citizens of the City of Man, he says, contend for the contrary. They follow the example of Adam and Eve and refuse to obey God's law, which is both eternal and made manifest in nature itself. They wish to establish a city *posthabito Deo: with God set aside*. That is a common participle in Leo's writings, *posthabitus*. It always refers to something or Someone whom we foolishly believe we can do without. We set God to the side, giving Him a nod on Sunday, if that. But to set aside the Lawgiver is not simply to set aside His laws. It is to set aside *law itself.*

The Freemasons, for example, were "Naturalists," a name rich with irony. They begin by setting God aside. But we cannot do that without getting everything wrong, including nature. The Naturalists begin by denying the personal action of God: "They deny that anything has been taught by God; they allow no dogma of religion or truth which cannot be understood by the human intelligence, nor any teacher who ought to be believed by reason of his authority" (HG, 90). But that means "they no longer consider as certain and permanent those things which are fully understood by the natural light of reason, such as certainly are — the existence of God, the immaterial nature of the human soul, and its immortality" (HG, 92). Notice that Leo believes in a *greater* field for human reason than do the Naturalists or their allies, the self-styled Rationalists! Remove the foundation, and the walls collapse. Remove the God of nature, and nature crumbles. Set to the side for the moment the heavenly virtues "which no one can exercise or even acquire without a special gift and grace of God." Even the "duties which have their origin in natural probity," says Leo, will lack a sound basis (HG, 93). "For if we set religion aside," he writes to the bishops of Canada on the subject of education, "there is no moral education worthy of the name, or of any effect whatever" (*Affari vos* [1897], 1332; translation mine).

Take away the truth of God the Creator, intimately involved in the natural order and calling man to a life beyond himself. Do as the Naturalists and the Freemasons desire, says Leo, and "there will immediately be no knowledge as to what constitutes justice and injustice, or upon what principle morality is founded" (HG, 93). He does not say we will become muddled. He says we will know nothing at all. People who believe in God and in the natural order, even if they do not possess the supernatural virtues of faith, hope, and charity, will still be able to see that human life is sacred; that a marriage is a contract between a man and a woman; that children belong to their parents and not to a government; that a man's property is his own.

What we are left with when we shoulder God aside, says Leo, is *inops*: utterly impoverished, unsound, easily swayed by impulses of passion. That is because human beings are fallen. It is a truth we ignore to our destruction. Because of the frailty that is a consequence of Original Sin, human nature is prone to vice, and therefore "for a virtuous life it is absolutely necessary to restrain the disorderly movements of the soul, and to make the passions obedient to reason" (*HG*, 94). Even the pagan philosophers knew that. So if we are to attain the highest good for which we enter into society—the perfection of virtue—we must have laws that oblige us *against* indulging our appetites. But a society premised upon the satisfaction of appetites, that sees nothing beyond the acquisition of material comforts, cannot conceive of such laws, or, even if they were conceivable, can have no way of obliging people to heed them, to take them to heart and make them their own. It can sometimes compel compliance, but it can never instill true obedience. So the people remain restrainedly bad, rather than good and free.

Two choices remain. One may confess that the premise is wrong, return to the truth, and build upon solid foundations. Or one may turn diabolical; that is, one may acknowledge that the "society" that results from a practical denial of God is prone to vices that the pagans themselves considered to be enervating, degrading, and unspeakable. But we will not call them vices anymore. Instead we proclaim that we *seek* such things. We will live by what we know in our hearts is a lie, and the deeper we try to sink that lie into oblivion, the more will it rankle and poison.

Can man fall to that depth of madness? Would not practicality, if nothing else, restrain him? But we forget that for every man who visits the whorehouse, there is a pander who profits by it. Certain vices redound to the benefit of ambitious people whose rule depends upon the degradation of others. Here is Leo, writing before the modern welfare state and its new slavery: "Since generally no one is accustomed to obey crafty and clever men so submissively as those whose soul is weakened and broken down by *the domination of the passions*, there have been in the sect of the Freemasons some who have plainly determined and proposed that, artfully and of a set purpose, the multitude should be satiated with a boundless license of vice, as, when this had been done, it would easily come under their power and authority for any acts of daring" (*HG*, 95; emphasis mine).

The phrase I have highlighted illustrates what Leo believes is at stake for the human soul, in a society that is no society, because God has been banished from its common life. We are subject to *cupiditatum dominatu*, the lordship of appetites. We trade one lord for another. Make divorce possible, and we will feel the terrible might of passion (*cupiditatum*; *Arcanum divinae*, 75). Forget that all authority derives from God, and we will suffer "the insatiable craving for things perishable," literally, a *cupiditas* for things that drift and flow away from us (*Inscrutabili*, 11). We will no longer be a people who "rule justly and moderately, submit in conscience to our duty, govern our passions by virtue, give to each his due, and do not touch what belongs to another" (*cupiditates*; *Cum Multa Sint* [1882], 2110; translation mine). We will grant to the multitude an authority it cannot possess, flattering them and inflaming many passions (*cupiditatum*;

Immortale Dei, 123). We will vitiate reason itself, because "the influence of the passions oftentimes takes away, or certainly at least diminishes, the capacity for grasping the truth" (*cupiditates*; *Sapientiae Christianae*, 192).

But that means we lose everything:

> Nature did not fashion society with intent that man should seek in it his last end, but that in it and through it he should find suitable aids whereby to attain to his own perfection. If, then, a civil government strives after external advantages merely, and the attainment of such objects as adorn life; if in administering public affairs it is wont to put God aside, and show no solicitude for the upholding of moral law; it defects woefully from its right course and from the injunctions of nature: nor should such a gathering together and association of men be accounted a commonwealth, but only a deceitful imitation and make-believe of civil organization. (SC, 181)

The State that pretends to do without God is no commonwealth, but a pretense: a *simulatio societatis*, a bad simulation of a society. Again, that is because man is made by God, in the image of God, for fulfillment in God. As man is, so must his society be: "The case of governments is much the same as that of the individual; they must also run into fatal issues, if they depart from the *way*" (T, 470).

The Blessings of a True Society

The good and wise Pope Leo never condemns an error without commending a truth. What would a true society look like? To illustrate what he means, I ask the reader to consider the famous painting *The Angelus* by Jean-François Millet.

It well deserves to be loved. A man and woman, farm folk hoeing potatoes, pause in their hard work to pray. The noonday sky casts a glow about them. On the earth we see the potatoes, some of them spilling out of a burlap sack. There's a wheelbarrow nearby, with a few full sacks on it. The man has doffed his wide-brimmed hat — wide-brimmed, for work in the sun — and holds it against his breast. The woman folds her hands in prayer. They bow their heads. Just visible upon the far horizon is the spire of a church. The title, *The Angelus*, brings all the motifs together. It is the moment of Emmanuel: *and the Word was made flesh, and dwelt among us* (John 1:14).

What would the secular mind understand about this scene? A man and woman are praying. That's their business, not ours. They're poor. They should be given public assistance. And that is all.

Let us understand more. First, we see that it is a man and a woman. They are married; the painter doesn't need to spell this out. They are Adam and Eve. They are made for one another, as God had ordained from the beginning, and therefore, says the Lord, alluding to that original society before the Fall, a man shall leave his mother and father and cleave unto his wife, and they two shall be one flesh.

To believe that this man and this woman should put themselves asunder to gratify their desires is to make nonsense of the painting and of the nature and the grace that Millet has portrayed. They are with and for one another, reflecting the abiding and never-swerving love of God for man. God does not renege on His promises. Mary does not regret saying, "Behold, I am the handmaid of the Lord." Jesus, our Emmanuel, abides with us until the end of time, most intimately in the Holy Sacrifice of the Mass.

Man, in the Image of God

The man and woman belong together, as Millet has shown in the form of their bodies. The husband is wiry, with broad, angular shoulders. The wife is about as tall as he is, with wide hips. They are poor — it's no gold coins they pry up from the furrows. They wear the peasant's wooden shoes, shoes that would rub their feet into a mass of blisters were it not for thick calluses years in the making. But they are not destitute. The woman's body suggests fruitfulness, the blessings of children to come.

Then there is the work. "You shall earn your bread by the sweat of your brow," says the Lord to Adam after the original sin (cf. Gen. 3:19). But the Catholic Church has never held that work is merely a curse. "Ora et labora," say the sons of Benedict: *pray and work*. All work may be ennobled by love; and work is a powerful prayer when performed for the glory of God.

We affirm the converse too. Unless it is done in love, work is mere toil and grows inhuman. If done to obscure the glory of God, it is demonic. Since man is a social being, his prayer and his work are also social. The man and the woman are united by both the prayer and the work, and it is indeed hard to distinguish those actions. The painting shows a pause in one kind of prayer for another kind of prayer, in one kind of work for another kind of work. Yet the overwhelming impression we gain from it is not of hurry or strain, but peace.

The Lord is present in this tilling the field and this song of praise. There's no false severance of the things of man from the things of God. Religion is not for Sunday alone; it is for every minute of our lives, and every fiber in our bodies, male and female, and every inch of the fields we work. "If the Lord does not build the house," says the psalmist, "they labor in vain that build it" (cf. Ps. 127:1). We may apply that maxim to any society whatsoever. Unless the Lord has built the house, there is no proper house for man to dwell in. There's no such thing, strictly speaking, as secular humanism: only *secular inhumanism*, man's organization of his world against God and therefore against himself. Abolish God, abolish man. There's no such thing as a secular society; only a secular collective, or grab bag, or metastatic tumor, for if human beings are not united from above, they cannot be truly united at all. Without God, man strives for his portion of finite things; and the deadly sins of pride, envy, avarice, and spiritual sloth ensure that we are never content with the heaps of nothings we have.

Finally, that steeple. The man and woman are praying because they hear the Angelus bell tolling from far away. This is no secret handshake, no skulking in a back room, no relegation of prayer and praise to a cordoned-off ecclesial space, barely tolerated by the "real" world of secularists, hedonists, and assorted idolaters of power and wealth and celebrity. The bell rings out over the village and the plains.

Why is that so important for the civil order? Pope Leo always asserts an analogy between the relationship of reason to faith and the relationship of the civil to the sacred. It's not a relationship between equals. Faith without reason may be feeble, or may be a holy child; but reason without faith can never be a child. Reason without faith is crippled at best and grows deformed and monstrous at worst, animated by the pride and passion of man. Without the arrow of faith, says Leo, liberty degenerates into license; and the civil order loses those benefits conferred by Christianity, benefits secured by "fortitude, self-control, constancy, and the evenness of a peaceful mind, together with many high virtues and noble deeds" (*AD*, 59). Indeed, the ancient pagans were not secular in our sense, "for in their heart and soul the notion of a divinity and the need of public religion were so firmly fixed that they would have thought it easier to have a city without foundations than a city without God" (*HG*, 97). I lay special stress upon these words. The Pope does not say that a city wherein faith is no part of civic life will be a bad city. He says it will be *no city*. It will be a simulacrum of a city, a political or cartographic fiction, a conglomerate of human activity without foundation and without aim.

The good things I have noted in Millet's painting are still insufficient to build up a Catholic social order. But they are necessary. We must affirm the holiness of marriage and its being grounded in our created nature. We must affirm the holiness of our labor, not to amass luxury, but to secure those modest provisions that make for contentment upon earth, that we may worship God with a free heart, endow our children, and give generously to those in need. The earth is fertile; and man, working the earth, brings it the more intimately and blessedly into the plan of God. So too the man and woman, in their fertility, cooperate in bringing into being a new child, whose end is to enjoy God's very life.

The Tallest Building of All

Leo's logic, if we accept his premises, is inexorable. If man is made by God and for God, and if man by nature is a social creature, then his social life too is made by God, for God. It too must be open to, even oriented toward, the divine. What we see on the horizon is not the towering glass of a money-making powerhouse, nor its cousin, the bold ramparts of a secular State, but a steeple — so frail a needle of faith and hope and love, against the ugly colossi of Babel.

Yet not so frail after all. That needle pierces the heavens like a prayer; it pierces the heart like the grace of God. When the

Truth came to dwell among us, says Leo, man awoke as from a dreary slumber. He saw once more that he was meant to live not for things that pass away, but for the everlasting God. That meant that every single human being was on the same exalted journey. "From this beginning," says Leo, "and on this foundation consciousness of human dignity was restored and lived again; the sense of a common brotherhood took possession of men's hearts; their rights and duties in consequence were perfected or established anew and virtues beyond the imagination or conception of ancient philosophy were revived" (*T*, 466).

The truth of this assertion is open to any honest mind. Outside of the ambit of the Christian faith and those nations nourished by it, where are there hospitals for the poor? What Muslim travels to Molokai to live with the lepers and minister to them? Where are the schools for the indigent? Where is the secular equivalent of St. Isaac Jogues, missionary to the Hurons, who came to bring them peace and a hope for things higher than life by pillage and slaughter, and who loved them so dearly that he returned to them after they had mutilated him, content to accept a cruel death at their hands? Christ did not come to earth to establish a secular State, but He could not have done more for any State than He did when He established the Church, for "wherever the Church has set her foot, she has straightway changed the face of things, and has attempered the moral tone of the people with *a new civilization,* and with virtues before unknown. All nations which have yielded to her sway have become eminent for their culture, their sense of justice, and the glory of their high deeds" (*ID*, 107; emphasis mine).

That new civilization is not an object so much as a virtue, a way of life: *nova urbanitas.* It does not depend upon technological sophistication, or material wealth, or the wisdom of statutes.

It changes the hearts of the people, turning them from ferocity to mildness, from the pursuit of things that cannot be shared without diminution, to the pursuit of things that grow greater by being shared. Leo quotes St. Augustine thus addressing the Church in grateful wonder: "Thou joinest together, not in society only, but in a sort of brotherhood, citizen with citizen, nation with nation, and the whole race of men, by reminding them of their common parentage. Thou teachest kings to look to the interests of their people, and dost admonish the people to be submissive to their kings. With all care dost thou teach all to whom honor is due, and affection, and reverence, and fear, consolation, and admonition and exhortation, and discipline, and reproach, and punishment. Thou showest that all these are not equally incumbent on all, but that charity is owing to all, and wrongdoing to none" (*ID*, 118; cf. Augustine, *De Moribus Ecclesiae Catholicae*, 30.6).

The Church achieves these things not merely by abstract teaching, but by her incarnate practice. She does not unite people of like mind in a party of opinion. She unites whole persons, in love of God and neighbor. Think again of the chapel. The peasant and his wife will not be the only ones pausing to pray the Angelus. And on a Sunday, they will be inside that chapel, made one with their neighbors in the Sacrament of the Altar. "Very beautiful and joyful too," writes Leo in *Mirae caritatis* (1902), his treatise on the Eucharist, "is the spectacle of Christian brotherhood and social equality which is afforded when men of all conditions, gentle and simple, rich and poor, learned and unlearned, gather round the holy altar, all sharing alike in this heavenly banquet" (MC, 529).

Consider: outside of that chapel, where do rich and poor meet as brothers? Where does the professor break bread with the janitor? Where does the politician bow his head beside the simpleminded thirty-year-old child, who surpasses him in real virtue and grace? Where does the manager of millions confess his utter poverty? Where is the mayor a minor? Where is the president a beggar? Where else does anyone hear, "Unless you become as these little children, you shall not enter the kingdom of heaven" (cf. Matt. 18:3)?

How else can we presume to bind people in a real society, with the felt bonds of brotherhood, outside of the Church of Jesus Christ? Peace on earth is not to be had without recourse to the Prince of Peace. Unity—as opposed to uniformity, conformity, conglomeration—derives from the Sacrament of Unity. "Some there are," says Leo, who, when they hear the Pope recommend the Eucharist as the solution for the troubles of our times, will turn aside with "a certain peevish disgust" (MC, 519). But that is only the result of pride, which darkens the mind and hardens the heart. For no sooner had the goodness of the Lord appeared among us, "than there at once burst forth a certain creative force which issued in a new order of things and pulsed through all the veins of society, civil and domestic," imparting a new direction "to government, to education, to the arts," and turning the minds of men "towards religious truth and the pursuit of holiness" (MC, 520).

Our society, said the Pope on the silver jubilee of his pontificate, in *Pervenuti all' anno* (1902), is *traviata*, astray, wayward, out of the right road. It must return to the Way, if it is to recover the way. For the Christian faith leavens both the individual and the society: "It assuages sorrow, it calms hatred, it engenders heroes" (566). The Church "has freed humanity from the yoke of slavery in preaching to the world the great law of equality and human fraternity" (PAA, 571). This equality, about which I will have more to say, is not ideological or political, but reaches to the core of man's being and demands reverence.

For Jesus Christ is *Liberator humani generis*, the Liberator of mankind (*Libertas Praestantissimum* [1888]). What does it mean to be free? To that we now turn.

2

Human Liberty

*But unto every one of us is given grace accord-
ing to the measure of the gift of Christ. Wherefore he saith, When he ascended up on high, he
led captivity captive, and gave gifts unto men.*
—Ephesians 4:7-8

*Thy word is a lamp unto my feet,
and a light unto my path.*
—Psalm 119:105

Virgil has led the poet Dante down through all the circles of Hell, until at the very bottom, the sinkhole of the world, they see Satan. He is no heroic rebel uttering blasphemies against God. He says nothing at all, at least not with his lips. He gnaws the three most notorious traitors in human history: Judas Iscariot, Brutus, and Cassius, in his three slavering mouths, a parody of the Trinity. There is no communication, not even the mockery of a society.

He does one thing more. He flaps his wings incessantly, with the dreadful changelessness of a machine. He is "free" to do so; no one else compels him. He is "free" to cease; but that would be to admit that his freedom comes not from himself but from his Creator. With every beat of his bat-like wings, Satan affirms the lie that he is his own, to will what he pleases. And with every beat of those wings, the gale they stir up blows, and the water of the miserable River Cocytus congeals as it reaches the bottom, and Satan and his fellow traitors remain locked in place, bound to the ice, just as their hearts are frozen in everlasting hatred and futility.

Modern man's view of freedom is the same that Satan asserts, and that Dante and almost the entire pagan and Christian tradition before him rejected. It is the sheer exercise of will. It is also a pure negative. I am "free" to the extent that the State *cannot* tell me that I *cannot* do as I please. A man racked upon the wheels of pornography, ruining his marriage and hollowing out his soul as he stares at the images in mingled fascination, boredom, loneliness, and disgust, that man is called "free," because no one is compelling him to do that, or because no one is preventing him from doing that. A woman's friend bursts into the room with the joyous news that she and her husband will be having a baby, and instead of sharing the joy, her friend grits her teeth, turns aside, and forces a smile, recalling that she exercised her "freedom" to have her child disposed of. She too is "free," as modern man sees it. For modern man's freedom is empty. It has no aim. It has no meaning. It is the false freedom of ennui and despair. Modern man boasts that he has no ties. Neither does a body in free fall.

Jesus Christ was not talking about that zero-freedom when He said that He was the Truth and that the truth would set men free (cf. John 8:32). We might add that such pagan philosophers as Plato, Aristotle, Cicero, Epictetus, Seneca, and Marcus Aurelius all insisted that liberty without virtue was a mirage. Virtue sets man free. Vice enslaves.

"There are many," says Pope Leo, "who imagine that the Church is hostile to human liberty," but that is because they have "a false and absurd notion as to what liberty is" (LP, 135). The adjectives Leo uses are *perverso* and *praepostero*: twisted inside out, and utterly backward, putting the tail where the head should be. Freedom cannot be mere permission. License is not simply a false version of liberty. It is the death of liberty.

That is because man's liberty is *for* his perfection. If you abuse your arms, tearing at them with hooks and crushing them under sledgehammers, you will not achieve any of the good that arms are for. If you abuse your free judgment and turn to vice, you will have a will that is to the soul no better than the torn and crushed arms are to the body. No better, and probably far worse.

There's more. If you define liberty not by what binds you to others, but by what ensures that you need not acknowledge any bond, then you have already denied your human nature. Leo expresses the constant wisdom of the Church when he affirms the *reality* of society — neither a numerical aggregate nor a collective — and when he sees this reality as rooted in man's nature, created by God. For it is God "who has made man for society, and has placed him in the company of others like himself, so that what was wanting to his nature, and beyond his attainment if left to his own resources, he might obtain by association with others" (*LP*, 150).

Leo, again, is thinking not only of material goods, as needful as these may be, but of moral and spiritual goods. For, as I've argued, the laws that men enact cannot oblige us simply on utilitarian grounds. We are not bound to a calculus of advantage. We are bound, in loyalty, to *persons*. "Authority," he writes, "is the one and only foundation of all law," and authority is of God (*LP*, 140). Laws that enjoin good and forbid evil "by no means derive their origin from civil society; because just as civil society did not create human nature, so neither can it be said to be the author of the good which befits human nature, or of the evil which is contrary to it" (*LP*, 141). This principle provides a check against the whims of ambitious men, whether they rule as monarchs or as party leaders in a democracy. We do not create law. We recognize it and embody it in our statutes: "Laws come before men live together in society."

Law is the prerequisite for genuine freedom. Leo's reasoning is plain. If freedom meant the capacity to choose anything at all, including evil, then God and the blessed angels would not be free. But *whosoever commits sin is the slave of sin* (cf. John 8:34). When man acts according to reason, "he acts of himself and according to his free will; and this is liberty. Whereas, when he sins, he acts in opposition to reason, is moved by another, and is the victim of foreign misapprehensions." Freedom is the unimpeded capacity to fulfill our God-ordained end. The conclusion: "The eternal law of God is the sole standard and rule of human liberty, not only in each individual man but also in the community and civil society which men constitute when united" (LP, 142).

Whatever laws we pass to secure the common good derive their legality, their *binding* character, from their being consonant with reason, and reason "prescribes to the will what it should seek after or shun, in order to the eventual attainment of man's last end, for the sake of which all his actions should be performed. This ordination of *reason* is called law" (LP, 139). If we were brute beasts, we would need no law. Our instincts would be our law. Precisely because we possess a free will, we are bound to submit to law, which curbs our inclination to evil and destruction, and guides us in the path of virtue and life. Human law, insofar as it is just, is an embodiment of the divine law. We do more than comply with it. We obey it: we "hear" it in our consciences, and take it to heart, for "lawful power is from God, *and whosoever resisteth authority resisteth the ordinance of God*" (LP, 144).

Moral Liberty and Political Liberty

Here many classical liberals will demur. They will say, "What are we to do when the government is unjust? You are asking us to submit tamely to an order which we would overturn, for the good of mankind. Your prescriptions are *politically* untenable."

Pope Leo gives such objectors four replies. The first is that the burden of proof, and it is quite heavy, must always rest with the innovators. The second is that such liberalism naturally leads to one form of tyranny or another. The third is that only a submission to divine law and authority provides a guard against ambitious men and all-devouring states. The fourth is that true liberty does more than protect societies; it *creates* them. Let us look at the first three in turn. I will devote a separate chapter to the fourth.

The first one may surprise us. Aren't all innovations devoutly to be wished? But consider the matter. The man who really loves his wife does not want a new one, nor will he always be pestering her to become other than she is. People who love their neighborhood do not, unless some physical or moral or financial hurricane has struck, desire to tear down its houses, fell the trees, block up the stream, and blacktop the park. If I am faithful to Holy Mother Church, the last thing I'd wish is to see her trumped up with gaudy new fashions to suit the political taste of the day. We should happily "yield obedience in all things to the teaching and authority of the Church, in no narrow or mistrustful spirit, but with [our] whole soul and promptitude of will" (*Praeclara gratulationis publicae*, 312). Even before I begin to consider the theology of it, there would be something suspicious in the craving for innovation. Innocent children love their homes and do not want to trade them in. It is only the bored and sin-burdened adult who can never rest contented anywhere.

In the old Roman republic, the most damning thing you could call a man was "innovator," and the second most damning thing was "ambitious." The former suggested a deep disdain for the traditions upon which the Romans had built their nation. The latter literally described what an unscrupulous man would do, going round and about, canvassing for votes. Pope Leo understood that Roman point of view.

So in his inaugural encyclical, *Inscrutabili* (1878), the Pope combines in one general condemnation the current "widespread

subversion of the primary truths on which, as on its foundations, human society is based," leading to obstinacy against
rightful authority, civil strife, contempt for law, craving (*cupiditas*) for things that flit away, "forgetfulness of things eternal,"
self-destruction, public corruption, traitors who cast themselves
as patrons of liberty, and, in short, "the deadly kind of plague
which infests society in its inmost recesses, allowing it no respite
and foreboding *ever fresh disturbances* and final disaster" (*I*, 9-10;
emphasis mine). Those ever fresh disturbances? *Novas rerum
conversiones*: literally, the new overturning of things.

So too runs his commitment to piety in *Quod apostolici
muneris*, a more specific encyclical against socialism, communism, and nihilism, what Leo saw as three forms of one disease.
The Church, he says, has long been fighting the same war, begun
against her "by the Reformers" (*Novatoribus*: the Innovators),
now growing in vehemence, "aimed at giving free course to the
rejection of all revelation, the subversion of the supernatural
order, and the enthronement of unaided reason, with its vagaries or rather ravings" (*QAM*, 24). They were motivated by the
"harmful and lamentable rage for innovation" (*rerum novarum
studia*: eagerness for new things), and now their work has borne
fruit in a false "*new jurisprudence* which was not merely previously
unknown, but was at variance on many points with not only the
Christian, but even with the natural law" (*ID*, 120). The Masons,
in their battle against the Church, have roused up the people by
"a thirst for novelty" (*rerum novarum*: new things), urging them
to assail both the Church and the civil power (*HG*, 100). The
very title of Leo's most celebrated work on the church's social
teaching, *Rerum novarum*, is a condemnation. For what is sweep-
ing the world is *rerum novarum cupidine*, the lust for new things,
or "the spirit of revolutionary change" (*RN*, 208).

What's wrong with that thirst for overturning old orders? Nothing necessarily, when the old order is not order at all but complete disorder, a violation of the law of God and of natural justice. But there must always be a strong presumption in favor of what our forefathers have handed down to us. Piety demands it. It is built into the nature of man. We do not live only in the times when we are breathing. The past is present to us still, and we will be present to our descendants yet to come. One of the bitterest expressions of despair in all of literature comes from the dying lips of the wicked cardinal in John Webster's *The Duchess of Malfi*: "Let me be laid by and never thought of." "I am forgotten as a dead man out of mind," says the psalmist in his distress (Ps. 31:12).

That is why Leo defends private ownership by referring not to economic utility, but to the time-transcending mode of being that distinguishes man from the beasts. Man has a right to have and hold things "in stable and permanent possession," for man, "fathoming by his faculty of reason matters without number, and linking the future with the present, becoming, furthermore, by taking enlightened forethought, master of his own acts, guides his ways under the eternal law and the power of God, whose providence governs all things" (*RN*, 211). For this reason he may justly claim "not only the fruits of the earth," but the one thing in our experience that is most stable and dependable, "the very soil," the land from which, ultimately, we derive all of the material goods that make civilization possible (*RN*, 212).

Since, therefore, the providence of God does not change, nor does the nature of good and evil, and since man himself, dwelling in time but rising above it by memory and forethought, looks ultimately toward the eternal, all those who insist upon the magic of fundamental change are deceiving themselves and others. And they are shackling man to the sole time in which he lives.

That is not only because they *cannot* change man's nature or God's law. It is also because the attempt to do so requires tyranny. A house built upon sand will fall—but before it falls, its builders will prop it up with all kinds of extrinsic and expensive supports. A State that rejects the natural law will fall—but before it falls, its subjects will be conscripted to brace themselves against its walls, whether they like it or not. Leo is relentless about this. Liberalism—atheism in civil matters—is one step from tyranny.

In part it is the tyranny of a depraved populace: "Nor can that be regarded as liberty which, shamefully and by the vilest means, spreading false principles, and freely indulging the sensual gratification of lustful desires, claims impunity for all crime and misdemeanor, and thwarts the goodly influence of the worthiest citizens of whatsoever class" (*I*, 12). For the Socialists, "preaching up the community of goods, declare that no one should endure poverty meekly, and that all may with impunity seize upon the possessions and usurp the rights of the wealthy" (*QAM*, 30).

In part it is the tyranny of any populace at all. For when it acknowledges no law above it, "a State becomes nothing but a multitude, which is its own master and ruler" (*ID*, 120), and then man must suffer "the supremacy of the greater number" (*LP*, 145). But that only fosters unruly desires, because then nothing is ever settled, and all lies within the power of the most fickle of all things, the mob. If yesterday's law is tomorrow's jest, what must that imply for today's law? The State's sovereignty will be merely "artificial," resting on "unstable and shifting bases, namely, the will of those from whom it is said to be derived," and therefore its laws will be "but the expression of the power of the greater number and the will of the predominant political party. It is thus that the mob is cajoled into seeking to satisfy its desires [*appetiti licenziosi*: licentious appetites]; that a loose rein is given to popular passion, even when it disturbs the laboriously acquired tranquility of the State" (*PAA*, 562).

But in the main it is that there will be no check against the growth of the State, and thus the second reply leads to the third. Where liberty is mistaken as license, the State, troubled as it will be, must grow. The State stands in for God. Some men will try to alter for their purposes the unalterable nature of marriage. The liberty of the Church will be curtailed, for the State will seek "either to forbid the action of the Church altogether, or to keep her in check and bondage to the State" (*ID*, 122), which for its part will without warrant begin to interfere "in municipal or family affairs" which are outside of its purview (*ID*, 128).

Indeed, if rulers and subjects understand that they are under one eternal law, that will be "an effectual barrier being opposed to tyranny," and "the authority in the State will not have all its own way, but the interests and rights of all will be safe-guarded—the rights of individuals, of domestic society, and of all the members of the commonwealth; all being free to live according to law and right reason," wherein "true liberty really consists" (*LP*, 144). A State that respects true liberty will keep itself within its proper bounds and not grow oppressive or morbid. But those bounds can be established only by what transcends the State, for "the Almighty alone can commit power to a man over his fellow-men" (*SC*, 185). Thus, far from there being an inevitable conflict between the civil and the religious, it is by religion alone that the State acts from authority, appealing to the hearts of men, rather than ruling by force. Religion keeps the State in its place—a place both worthy of honor and sub-ordinate to man's higher destiny.

Religion also keeps us from making an idol out of the *form* that the State takes. People charge the Church with being "jeal-ous of modern political systems," but that, says Leo, is "a ridicu-lous and groundless calumny," *inanis et ieiunia*, empty and starved, meaningless and flimsy. Leo writes to the American bishops in admiration of the wise and virtuous father of our country, George Washington, who granted to Catholics a respect that many oth-ers among the Founders would not have given. He understands that the Church should recognize what is noble in the American love for democracy, for the Church "has never disregarded the manners and customs of the various nations which it embraces" (*Testem benevolentiae*, 444). In fact, Leo seems to have felt quite a warm affection for our still new America, as he confesses him-self happy for the chance "of regarding with admiration that exceptional disposition of your nation, so eager for what is great, and so ready to pursue whatever might be conducive to social progress and the splendor of the State" (*TB*, 441).

But the Catholic is not compelled to believe that democracy is the finest form of government there is. He is not compelled to do that, because it is not necessarily true in the abstract, and it is cer-tainly far from true in its concrete realizations. So much the less, then, can Leo accept democracy as a norm for the Church. For "the Master and exemplar of all sanctity is Christ, to whose rule all must conform who wish to attain to the thrones of the blessed. Now, then, Christ does not at all change with the progress of the ages, but is *yesterday and today, and the same forever*" (*TB*, 449). We will discuss this at greater length in a chapter to come.

And it is Christ, not democracy, much less the mechanics of elections, who has set us free. Free for what purpose? To attain our human and superhuman ends; and, by our very nature, we are meant to do that within a society. What, then, is a society? Let us now turn, as Leo does, to the first natural society of mankind: the marriage of man and woman.

3

Marriage

*But from the beginning of the creation God made
them male and female. For this cause shall a man
leave his father and mother, and cleave to his wife;
and they twain shall be one flesh; so they are no
more twain, but one flesh. What therefore God
hath joined together, let not man put asunder.*
—Mark 10:7-9

*Thou following criedst aloud, "Return, fair Eve!
Whom fliest thou? Whom thou fliest, of him thou art,
His bone, his flesh; to give thee being I lent
Out of my side to thee, nearest the heart,
Substantial life, to have thee by my side
Henceforth an individual solace dear;
Part of my soul I seek thee, and thee claim
My other half." With that thy gentle hand
Seized mine, I yielded, and from that time see
How beauty is excelled by manly grace,
And wisdom which alone is truly fair.*

—John Milton, *Paradise Lost*, 4.750-757

I t is not good for the man to be alone," said God (Gen. 2:18),
when Adam had named the beasts and found none among
them to be a fit companion for him. So then He caused a deep
sleep to overcome the man, and fashioned from his side, "nearest the heart," as the poet Milton says, a woman to be that
companion.

Let's pause to notice a few things about the account in Genesis. The sacred author cannot have been under any confusion
about whether a man can engender the generations on his own.
When God made the beasts of the field, He made them male
and female, and blessed them, saying, "Increase and multiply"
(cf. Gen. 1:22). But the author, under the inspiration of the
Holy Spirit, sets the creation of woman apart from the creation
of the sexes in the animal kingdom. Then the woman must be
more than a physical mate for the man. She is his "helpmeet,"
in Hebrew his *'ezer*, a word often used to describe the gracious
action of God, who is our *'ezer* and our salvation. Thus, the
society of man and woman together is different from the casual
mating of the beasts.

It is instead a reflection of the inner life of God.

"Let us make man in our image," says God (Gen. 1:26), mys-
teriously using, for the first time in Scripture, the first person
plural. Christians see in that plural an adumbration of the Trinity.
If that is so, we may say that without woman, or rather without

the union of man and woman in marriage, there is something still lacking in the image of God that we are to embody and make manifest. The three-personed God we worship is Himself a society of love; and the prime society He creates is the marriage between man and woman. That human society in turn is the foundation of all other societies, as the pagan Aristotle observed. The family and the household come first. The State comes later, both in time and in order of being. And just as the family is *for* its members, both individually and together, so the State is *for* families, individually and together.

Pope Leo understood these principles, which were often denied or derided by the revolutionaries of his time, and which are still denied or derided by many among us now, who accept as a matter of course the all-competent headship of the State or the all-determining individual will.

Can, for instance, Christian marriage flourish in a State that gives its blessings to arrangements that Western societies have always considered at best irregular, and at worst reprehensible? Or are Christians free to give their tacit blessing also to such arrangements? Not unless they wish to cast their lot with idolaters. For the secularists of Leo's time desired to bring marriage "within the *contracted sphere* of those rights which, having been instituted by man, are ruled and administered by the civil jurisprudence of the community" (*AD*, 67; emphasis mine). Leo's words are *exiguum gyrum*, literally, the *tiny round*, the *negligible arena*. Let's think about that for a moment. There are rights that we possess because we have been made by God, for God. Those rights touch upon our *being* itself. They are as deep as the seas and as high as the stars above. Then there are "rights," or rather permissions, granted to us by the State in which we live; let us say, the right to a free public education for our children. Those things are called rights by analogy. They are what the community has agreed to guarantee. But they are few, contingent, and of narrow scope.

Leo reveals what such statists really are, in a sentence of impressive perspicacity: "All those who reject what is supernatural, as well as all who profess that they worship above all the divinity of the State, and strive to disturb whole communities with such wicked doctrines, cannot escape the charge of delusion" (*AD*, 68). They ignore *what marriage really is*, regardless of what any State or any individual may imagine about it. Such knowledge was available even to the ancient pagans: "Innocent III, therefore, and Honorius III, our predecessors, affirmed not falsely nor rashly that a certain sacredness of marriage existed ever amongst the faithful and unbelievers," all of whom regarded marriage "as conjoined with religion and holiness." To believe that marriage can be subject to the definition of the State is to elevate the State to the throne of an idol.

But Christian marriage, writes Leo, "not only looks to the propagation of the human race, but to the bringing forth of children for the Church, *fellow-citizens with the saints, and the domestics of God, so that a people might be born and brought up for the worship and religion of the true God and our Savior Jesus Christ*" (*AD*, 64; translator's emphasis; cf. Eph. 2:19, and *Catechisma Romana*, 100.8).

Let's not dismiss that as the talk of piety. If we attend to Leo's thought, we will see that marriage is both a society in its own right and a cause of society. The good marriage, Leo says, will raise "a race of citizens animated by a good spirit and filled with reverence and love for God, recognizing it their duty to obey those who rule justly and lawfully, to love all, and to injure no one." And that is no accident.

For the marriage is, on earth, the paradigmatic society. If we can determine why this is so, we will see that the errors of the socialist and of the individualist libertarian are *the same error*. They commit the error by rejecting one or both of the faces of Jesus' great commandment: "Thou shalt love the Lord thy God with all thy heart and soul and mind and strength, and thou shalt love thy neighbor as thyself" (Luke 10:27). They misconceive what it means to be a *human individual* and a *human society*.

What if marriage were to be, as some want the Church herself to be, merely a "voluntary association of citizens," conforming itself, as some want the Church to conform herself, to the pattern of the times? If that pattern is individualistic, then Mr. Jones and Mrs. Jones, entering into the contract for their individual needs or desires, create nothing beyond themselves, even if they beget children; that is no true society. It is also not fully human. Made as we are in God's image, we *must love in order to become human*; it is not good for the man to be alone. The husband is for the wife. The wife is for the husband. They together are for their children. It would be as absurd for the husband or the wife to claim "rights" separate from their spouse as it would be for Christ to desire to set aside a space for Himself apart from the Father.

"He who would save his life must lose it," says Jesus (cf. Matt. 16:25), and that applies not only to our salvation, but to all healthy human societies. To insist, as feminists do, that a woman's choices in certain matters have nothing to do with her husband is like insisting, as did the men who questioned Jesus about marriage, that a man should be able to dismiss his wife without consulting her. Beneath all of this, there is nothing noble at all, only self-love. And that, Leo writes in *Exeunte iam anno* (1880), is inimical to society itself, which demands the generosity of self-restraint and the discipline of self-giving: "Will anyone be inclined to do right who has been accustomed to make self-love the sole rule of what he should do or avoid doing? No man can be high-souled, or kind, or merciful, or restrained who has not learned to conquer self, and to despise all worldly things when opposed to virtue" (171). "They call self-love liberty," says Leo, of the rich and heedless socialists of his day (*EIA*, 170).

This rejection of self-love also explains why the human society can never be an aggregate. For the human society, unlike the ants in an anthill, is a whole not made up of parts, but of wholes: each human person is, in the order of being, infinitely greater than all the rest of the physical universe. For each human person, Christ died upon the Cross. Each human person is made in the image of God. St. Paul's more-than-metaphor comparing Christians to the parts of a body makes sense *only if it is the Body of Christ*. An anthill can spare a hundred ants to save the whole. A surgeon may cut off a gangrenous toe to save the whole. But a family that would "sacrifice" the good of one of its members for the whole is not a family, but a criminal syndicate, caught in the bonds of self-love. The human society *is for that social creature, the human person*, not to promote his self-love, but to promote his fulfillment as a human being. The husband is for the wife, not that she may do as she pleases, but that she may do as she ought, in the bonds of divine love and human love that alone set us free. The wife is for the husband, not that he may do as he pleases, but that he may come to know that same freedom.

This is why the Church, although stuffed to the rafters with sinners, is the perfect society. She knows that she will be judged by her love even for the least of all, the scoundrels, the ignorant, the poor, the unborn. She dare not give over a single one of them, not one little child in the womb, in a trade for all the good opinion of the world. She is *for man by being for God alone*; she is that, or she is nothing.

The advocates of a collective believe that, as by the magic of some economic god, the individual persons within it will somehow thrive, despite the fact that they are no longer regarded as individuals but as counters in the vast plan. The advocates of a libertarian atomism believe that, as by the magic of the same economic god wearing a different hat, the "society" will somehow thrive, despite the fact that everyone will be acting out of self-love, and let the society go hang. Sometimes these advocates intermingle, so that we have the phenomenon of the collectivist preaching atomism with regard to sex, which results in handing more and more power to the managers of the collective, or, less common, the atomist preaching the good of the armed collective, mobilized to make the world safe for atomism. But if we are not talking about the love of God (however imperfectly realized), and the love of man ordained by and for that love, we have in mind not only the wrong societies, but no societies at all. Temporary partnerships in vice, maybe, but nothing social, and nothing enduring.

There's a further implication for the Church. The Church can be true to man only by being true to Christ. But Christ demands our all, and He does not change with our changing times, as Leo reminds the fractious Americans who wished to make the Church more like their nation. "Christ does not at all change with the progress of the ages, but is *yesterday and today, and the same forever*" (*TB*, 449). He does not build in His Church a room where she can be herself, apart from Him, because it is only in her love for Him that she is a Church at all. That is simply to say *that Christ and the Church are wedded* and form one flesh.

That means that what we've come to call "cafeteria Catholicism" is essentially antisocial. Imagine what it would be like to drive on a highway if everyone had agreed to obey only half of the rules of the road, and no telling, from driver to driver, which ones. Imagine what kind of "marriage" it would be if the spouses decided to keep only those vows they pleased or when they pleased. That's the case of the person who agrees to keep a part of the Gospel: "For they who take from Christian doctrine what they please lean on their own judgments, not on faith, and not *bringing into captivity every understanding unto the obedience of Christ*, they more truly obey themselves than God" (*Satis cognitum* [1896], 368; cf. 2 Cor. 10:5).

Therefore those who claim to be obeying the social teaching of the Church while flouting her teaching on the family or the priesthood not only do not really understand the social teaching of the Church; they are being antisocial, seeking to dismember the Body of Christ — or to take His spouse out for a night on the town, for self-fulfillment, or whatever the silly phrase of the day may be.

Building upon a Solid Foundation

The reader may well ask when I propose to come around to discussing economics, which is the only thing most people consider when they hear the phrase *social justice*. They mean by *economics* not what it means in the Greek, or in the common-sense Aristotelian and Thomistic philosophy that Leo championed — that is, "the governance of the household" — but rather political issues regarding wages and employment. We will have that discussion. But we cannot put up a roof without walls, or walls without a foundation. Or, more precisely, we must recover the knowledge that economics in the abstract modern sense is supposed to be *for economics in the fundamental and personal sense.*

That is why Pope Leo never speaks about economics without directing his steady gaze at the household and the family, the love of man and woman bound in holy matrimony and the children they raise. It isn't that a society is made up of families as a factory is made up of bricks. Families are not parts. They are small but integral human societies; they deserve our reverence just as each member within them deserves our reverence. Each Christian family too is a domestic church. When St. Paul said that wives must reverence their husbands and husbands must love their wives, he wasn't just giving practical advice on how to maintain harmony under the roof. He was affirming the real analogy in being, between Christian marriage and the union of Christ with His Bride, the Church, which is the perfect society, the perfect fellowship of love. Therefore, laws that strike at the holiness of marriage attack the heart of the Church and of civil society.

The laws allowing for divorce in Leo's time were far less irresponsible than ours, but Leo already sees their corruption at work. Thus he writes in *Inscrutabili*:

> When impious laws, setting at naught the sanctity of this great sacrament, put it on the same footing with mere civil contracts, the lamentable result followed, that, outraging the dignity of Christian matrimony, citizens made use of legalized concubinage in place of marriage; husband and wife neglected their bounden duty to each other; children refused obedience and reverence to their parents; the bonds of domestic love were loosened; and, alas! the worst scandal and of all the most ruinous to

public morality, very frequently an unholy passion opened the door to disastrous and fatal separations. (18)

It is a theme he will revisit throughout his long pontificate. Good laws teach, and so do bad laws. Good laws assist us in the difficult pursuit of virtue. Bad laws thwart that pursuit and encourage vice. The bad law that allows for "disastrous and fatal separations," that is, divorces, is like a rotten trunk, Leo says, from which only "worthless fruits" can come. The disease that breaks out within the home spreads its "cruel infection to the hurt and injury of individual citizens." When domestic life is Christian, the members of that society of the hearth will learn the habits of piety and obedience and mutual service, "to the restraint of that insatiable seeking after self-interest alone, which so spoils and weakens the character of men."

We'd do well to think hard upon that last sentence. The secularists among us, of both right and left, have nothing whereupon to build their vain dreams of society, but "enlightened self-interest," which the Pope has just nailed as a contradiction in terms. It's as if one were to talk about "responsible vice" or "humane cruelty." He has drawn a connection between selfishness and selfishness. The self-styled innovator who conceives of civil society only in material terms is the same man who will not abide Christian marriage. In both ways he spoils the character of the people; and we now see this spoiling among the materially wealthy and the materially poor, both destitute of the riches of a Christian home, both alienated from their fellow men and from God.

Let me put it as bluntly as I can. *Divorce violates the social teaching of the Church.* Laws that facilitate divorce are socially destructive. If that is true, then all the more may we say that *concubinage and fornication violate the social teaching of the Church*: men and women rightly instructed about the nobility of the sacrament would not "anticipate their marriage by a series of sins drawing down upon them the wrath of God" (*AD*, 81). Laws that encourage such things are socially destructive. To train young people in "safe" concubinage and fornication is to plant the deadly virus in the very heart.

Antisocial Divorce

Let us look at the matter more closely. The great error of most economic thinking these days is not that it is too keenly focused on the economy, but that it has all but forgotten it. A good friend of mine, a wise theologian, has encouraged his students to distinguish between what Aristotle calls *chrematistike*, the craft of amassing wealth, which Aristotle and Plato and the Stoics and the early Christians all viewed with a healthy suspicion, and *economike*, the laws governing the management of an *oikos*, a household. Another way to put this is that man is not made for an economy, but economy is made for man, who is ineluctably a *social* being, or, as Aristotle put it, a *political* being.

Aristotle did not mean that man is made for the charade of self-government that Americans enjoy every four years, with its heaves of moronic marketing, evasion, and dishonesty. Aristotle is the pagan with the flat feet. He stands squarely on the ground of common things. A *political* animal is a rational creature who thrives best within a *polis*, a smallish community of people who do not suffer edicts from afar, but who adjust their civil laws to the laws of man's nature, to secure among themselves the common good.

But mass politics overwhelms the *polis*. Let me give an example. In many places in Canada, what used to be self-governing towns have been swallowed up, for the sake of supposed efficiency, into enormous "units" or "municipalities," reducing almost to zero the authority of any single household or local groups of households or their schools. In the United States, there is no issue too personal or local that cannot be adjudicated by nine lawyers in a marble building in Washington. Mass politics joins in alliance with mass "economics" or chrematistics, whether of the left or the right, which ignores what man is made for. Opposed to both of these is society properly conceived, fashioned by healthy and thriving households.

Catholic social teaching will not allow us the ease of abstraction, as if "society" could denote any aggregate of human beings organized (or disorganized) according to any financial and, for want of a better word, political laws whatsoever. In short, a society must be social. It must be based upon the human good of friendship and what the medieval English called *neighborhood*, meaning the virtue of getting along with and assisting those among whom we live most closely. An economy too must be economic. It must be based on the good of households and must aim, although sometimes in an intricate or circuitous way, at that same good.

We cannot make any headway in understanding the encyclicals of Pope Leo unless we keep these things firmly in mind. The Pope's teachings on the nature of man, his eternal destiny, the sanctity of marriage, the good of the family, and social and economic justice are all one coherent and harmonious vision. We see as much in his encyclical on Christian marriage, *Arcanum divinae* (1880), for this too is eminently a *social* letter.

Leo begins by observing that Christ came among us, as Saint Paul says, "to re-establish all things" (cf. Eph. 1:10) in Him — *all things*, not just the Sunday things, as it were. Just as, in *Aeterni*

Patris, Leo affirmed the assistance that faith lends to reason, elevating it to heights it could never have scaled on its own, while reason in turn clarifies faith and protects it from lapsing into error, so too this new instauration in Christ "imparted a new form and fresh beauty to all things, taking away the effects of their time-worn age" (*AD*, 58). That refreshment came in the order of nature also, redounding to the good of nations and families. "The authority of rulers," he writes, "became more just and revered; the obedience of the people more ready and unforced; the union of citizens closer; the rights of dominion more secure" (*AD*, 59). The Christian faith could hardly have done more to procure the truly good things of a common life, had it been instituted solely for that purpose. It stands squarely against the tyranny both of rulers and of anarchists; of unjust laws, of unruly passions, and of the vain imaginations of ambitious men who would play the god over their fellow human beings.

Such is the context for Leo's discussion of marriage—and marriage, in turn, is the context for his economic and political thinking. Again, he observes that marriage is not a human creation, much less a creation of the State. Marriage is of divine origin. Its fruition is not in the satisfaction of individual desires, as potent or as harmless as some of those may be. Because it is divine, marriage is by necessity oriented toward the being of God Himself. Its fruitfulness participates in His creative bounty. Its unity reflects the inner life of love that is the Trinity. Its exclusivity and perpetuity reflect His faithfulness and His eternity. A State that pretends it can alter not the *conditions* of marriage but its very *nature* presumes upon the prerogatives of God. Nor is it *possible*, let alone permissible, for Christians to enter into a marriage that is strictly civil, says Leo, because the dignity of the sacrament inheres in it nonetheless: its sacramental quality is *intimamente essenziale*, of the most intimate essence (*Il Divisamento di sancire* [letter to the Bishop of Verona, February 8, 1893], 1128).

When Jesus teaches us that the two great commandments are like unto one another, we are apt to remember that we cannot love God aright unless we love our neighbor; but we are apt to forget that our love of neighbor cannot be divorced from the love we owe to God. If, then, we sin against marriage, demoting it to the status of a contract that in pagan times could be abrogated by the husband at a whim (and which now can be so abrogated by either husband or wife), we sin against God and neighbor both. We sow dissolution in what should be a society but degenerates into a mass, an aggregate, a confounding of wills.

Thus, according to Leo, it was an act of the highest mercy and justice at once when Jesus blessed marriage at Cana and went on to bring back "matrimony to the nobility of its primeval origin," in His role as "supreme Lawgiver" (*AD*, 62). We misread things if we assume that only a prohibition against divorce is involved. The marriage of man and woman, grounded in their biological, earthly nature, is divine in origin and end. It is the sphere in which most of us will be called to holiness, with a procreation both physical and spiritual: "By the command of Christ, [marriage] not only looks to the propagation of the human race, but to the bringing forth of children for the Church, *fellow-citizens with the saints, and the domestics of God*" (*AD*, 64; Eph. 2:19). Leo is ever at pains to show that the Church does for the State what the State cannot well do for itself. She makes citizens of the City of God, citizens who make for something like a just city here below.

If we consider the matter carefully, we see not only that Christian marriage is the foundation for a genuine society. It is a society in itself and a model for the society at large. Thus, when Leo describes the inner dynamic of a Christian marriage, it is in social terms. "The mutual duties of husband and wife have been defined," he writes, "and their several rights accurately established. They are bound, namely, to have such feelings for one another as to cherish always very great mutual love, to be ever faithful to their marriage vow, and to give one another an unfailing and unselfish help" (*AD*, 64). The key words here are *mutual* and *several*. They have profound implications for all genuine Catholic teaching on the just society.

We have almost lost the sense of *gift* implied by the word *mutual*. For us, it means that if John does something, then Mary does the same, and so on, until the end of time. We take it to imply a flat identity. But the inner meaning of the word involves an exchange of gifts, a reciprocity that is not arithmetical but human. Thus, the mutuality of the love between husband and wife is implied in their *several* or separate, distinct duties. It is precisely because the husband and wife are *not the same* in their mode of being human and even in their physical relations to one another that they can most fully embody the complete gift of self that love demands. Each complements the other; each completes the other, and this completion is not subjective but an objective, incarnate fact. The two are one flesh. The man is for the woman, the woman for the man, and both, as individuals and as a married couple, are for God.

From Christian marriages, says Leo, "the State may rightly expect a race of citizens animated by a good spirit and filled with reverence and love for God, recognizing it their duty to obey those who rule justly and lawfully, to love all, and to injure no one" (*AD*, 73). What, by contrast, might we expect from an anti-society of self-will and divorce? For some hedonists delight in riches, and others delight in sex, and still others in prestige or ease or nervous excitements. Are we to believe that men who are shameless and shiftless in the most intimate and most socially productive of human relations will be animated by civic responsibility and love of neighbor in their other public actions, where their duties are less clear and the opportunities for self-serving almost limitless?

Every sin against marriage is a sin against the very possibility of any kind of society at all. Every Christian marriage begun in purity and continued in faithfulness and duty and love is an exemplar for all social relations and allows us to imagine something better than the loneliness of self-will "wedded," in ghastly symbiosis, to the inhumanity and insanity of economics without households, and a State without citizens.

No Family, No Society

We may therefore assert here a principle that, if one troubles to read Scripture, the encyclicals of the popes, and the decrees of ecumenical councils, is unassailable. It is this: there is an inner identity between Catholic teaching on sex and Catholic teaching on society.

Pope Leo is quite clear on these matters. "The family," he writes in *Sapientiae Christianae*, "may be regarded as the cradle of civil society, and it is in great measure within the circle of family life that the destiny of the State is fostered" (206). Why should this be so? It is not, in Catholic thought, simply because families produce children. It is rather dependent upon the nature and meaning of the marital act itself.

When a man and a woman give their bodies to one another, their very nakedness testifies that it is a total gift. It is strange, this inherent meaning of the bodily relation. It's of no use to say,

"The act means what we take it to mean." That cannot be. If we do not intend the total gift, nevertheless we have to pretend that we intend it if but for a few minutes, merely to perform the act. And we do pretend it. We reveal ourselves to one another in our nakedness, which proclaims, "This is what I am," and, in the very vulnerability of the act, in our release, we declare, "This is all I have; I hold nothing back." No doubt we can imagine ourselves into passion, or we can pretend, while in the throes of a genuine passion, that it means only what it means for the fleeting moment — as if we were creatures without memory, and as if the act were only instantaneous.

But it is not, and we know it. It is the principal action whereby a man and a woman cooperate in the providential design of God for the human race. When the man and the woman commit their bodies to one another in this fashion, they make "one flesh," and *not* only for the moment. They know, regardless of how hard they may try to forget it, that they are doing what their parents did, and their parents before them. They are doing what brought them into being. And they are doing what, by its nature, is meant to bring *new* generations into being. Yes, they may try to thwart that result, just as they may try to feign passion while pondering ways to extricate themselves from the entanglement, or as they may try to separate the pleasure of the act and its emotional intensity from its biological meaning. None of that matters. The liar knows, somewhere in his heart, that he is lying. So do the unmarried people playing house with one another. They are doing something that unites human beings across the sexes and across the generations. It is *social* and not merely private.

To pretend otherwise is to introduce into the relations between men and women, into family life, and ultimately into all social relations, a corrosive and enslaving notion of autonomy. Those who shrug at fornication, which is a kind of false marriage with inbuilt divorce, should consider what Leo, in *Arcanum divinae*, has to say about the evils of unrestrained desires: "When the Christian religion is rejected and repudiated, marriage sinks of necessity into the slavery of man's vicious nature and vile passions, and finds but little protection in the help of natural goodness. A very torrent of evil has flowed from this source, not only into private families, but also into States" (73). The lie, that sexual intercourse is a private matter between two people, and that fornication and divorce, with their approval of dissolution in both senses of the word—loose living and the dissolving of a bond—are of no social consequence, is based upon an antipathy toward those now unfashionable virtues that make society possible in the first place. So Pope Leo: "Very many, imbued with the maxims of a false philosophy and corrupted in morals, judge nothing so unbearable as submission and obedience; and strive with all their might to bring about that not only individual men, but families also, nay indeed, human society itself, may in haughty pride despise the sovereignty of God" (*AD*, 67). Lest we think that such a society can survive, the Pope, heir to millennia of history of pagan and Christian civilizations, says most forthrightly, "Nothing has power to lay waste families and destroy the mainstay of kingdoms as the corruption of morals" (*AD*, 74-75).

That, for Pope Leo, is no broad generalization, but a conclusion based upon a shrewd reading of history and insight into the heart of man. Sexual sin is disruptive. People who cannot form those societies called families will end up living in chaos or will have to be managed by an ambitious and totalitarian State. Decades before Aldous Huxley satirized the soulless pursuit of infertile sexual pleasure, Pope Leo observed that vice, and the corrupting of marriage and the family, would make men prone to the designs of the ambitious and unscrupulous (*HG*, 95). In his brilliant analysis of family-hating academicians, *Utopia Against the Family*, Bryce Christensen says essentially the same thing: "Claiming that they are merely freeing people from an outmoded morality, modern political activists often use the rhetoric of liberation as a solvent for weakening personal commitment to families, so creating a mass of rootless individuals unable to resist the absolute claims of the utopian state."

To uphold sexual virtue is to uphold the possibility of a coherent society, and not as the result of a long and tenuous train of causes. Rather, there can no more be a genuine society without strong and stable families, than there can be a human body without bones. And those strong families cannot be built upon the quicksand of individual passions, shifting from time to time, nor upon the serpentine meanderings of the lie. I cannot make a habit of uttering, with my body, the lie that I give my all, now and forever, without that lie becoming also a habit of *being*: without my becoming the sort of person who may not be telling lies at the moment, but who reserves to himself the right to tell them again when it becomes convenient.

Even the right to hold property, in Pope Leo's thinking, is to be upheld not principally because it conduces to the pleasure or the autonomy of the individual holding it, but because without it the family could not exist. If we choose, we may remain virgins, and hold property as individuals; but all the more is it our right to hold property if we are the heads of families. To read Pope Leo's *Rerum novarum* is to be in the presence of someone who does not reduce all human questions to those of partisan politics and who emphatically does not believe in the ultimacy of the State. Consider this passage: "No human law can abolish the natural and original right of marriage, nor in any way limit the chief and principal purpose of marriage, ordained by God's authority from the beginning, *Increase and multiply*. Hence we have the family; the 'society' of a man's house—a society limited indeed in numbers, but no less a true 'society,' anterior to every kind of State or nation, invested with rights and duties of its own, totally independent of the civil community" (*RN*, 214).

The "society of a man's house"—Leo's words are *societas domestica*—figures constantly into the Pope's thinking. Youths must be trained in morality from within "the circle of home life," *domestica societate* (*I*, 17). Socialists, communists, and nihilists weaken the bond between man and woman, whereby "family life," *domestica societas*, "is chiefly maintained," and submit instead to lust (*QAM*, 23). "The family circle itself," *domestica societas*, feels the salutary influence of the Church, and is "the starting point of every city and every State" (*QAM*, 28). Christ gave us "power to attain holiness in the married state," and "made the natural union," *societatem*, "of one man with one woman far more perfect through the bond of heavenly love" (*AD*, 63), giving to that "marriage union," *nuptiali societati*—literally, the nuptial society—"a higher and nobler purpose than was ever given previously to it" (*AD*, 64). Those who "would break away from Christian discipline are working to corrupt family life"—*corrumpere societatem domesticam*—"and to destroy it utterly, root and branch" (*SC*, 206). American bishops must bravely proclaim the "Christian dogma of the indissolubility of marriage; which supplies the firmest bond of safety not merely to the family," *societatis domesticae*, "but to society at large" (*Longinquae oceani*, 330).

A group that destroys the goodness and individuality of its members is no true society, but a sickly cult. Just so, a "society" that destroys the integrity of families and robs them of their independence is no true society, but an oppressor, a parasite, a cancer. A healthy body supports the health of its members. All the more, then, must a State support the health of families, because, although in a sense families are "members" of a State, they are not, as fingers are to the hand or the hand to the body, parts of the State, without a life of their own.

It is instead as Pope Leo says: the family enjoys a priority over the State. The State in a sense is the creation of the family, and not the other way around. Hence, the family possesses rights that the State does not confer upon it but must recognize and defer to: "The contention, then, that the civil government should at its option intrude into and exercise intimate control over the family and the household, is a great and pernicious error," for "paternal authority can neither be abolished nor absorbed by the State; for it has the same source as human life itself" (*RN*, 215). Likewise, "the child takes its place in civil society, not of its own right, but in its quality as member of the family in which it is born" (*RN*, 216). Families are not wards of the State. The State is rather something created by families, and it must answer to them, and not the other way around.

Once we see the inner coherence of Catholic teaching on sex and the proper ordering of goods in society, we begin to suspect that the fantasy recommended by some among us—that we can have any kind of real society, just or otherwise, based upon sexual license—rests upon a mass of confusion. Everything is related. So if you are talking about the economy, the "law of the household" but not about mother and father and children; or if you are talking about poverty of income but not about moral destitution; or if you are talking about sexual ethics but not about marriage, and time and eternity; then you are not talking as a Catholic, but as someone who has forgotten that God's laws are not separable one from another. You may try out your nostrums with the simpleminded, but not to anyone who has actually read what our authorities have to say.

As Little Children

I'd like to end this chapter with an illustration. It comes not from the Church but from nature. I know that Norman Rockwell is an easy target for contempt, but, just as I have not managed to acquire a taste for the hideous, the squalid, the perverse, the chaotic, and the stupid in art, so have I not trained myself away from an affection for this man's paintings. I have in mind now one of his Four Seasons illustrations. It features a boy and a girl, about ten or eleven years old, just when the attraction of the opposite sex is awakening, but while it is still largely expressed in the innocent play of children.

In winter they're on a sled, the boy in back, hollering for glee, the girl in front, both feet stuck out to keep the sledding fast, while a goofy dog chases them, barking. In summer they're on a swing hung from a tree, both of them barefoot, the dog in the girl's lap, the boy standing in back, the girl making an O with her mouth as they sweep into the air, as carefree as babies. In fall they're walking to school, he still barefoot, looking just a little morose, while the dog follows behind. But the spring picture is the sweetest of the four, and, as always when Rockwell is at his best, it suggests a whole world of natural but profound human feeling.

The boy and girl are barefoot. He's wearing his straw hat, which casts his countenance in a suggestive shadow; and he's looking intently at the girl, while he holds a buttercup under her chin. She leans forward, arms behind her back, her eyes shut.

We know, without being told, that this scene is *right*. The boy and the girl are *for one another*. They are alone in all four pictures, but they are not alone. They are a part of the good and lovely world of trees and snow and weedy flowers and dogs. They go to school, so they are part of that social world also. But in their seedling love, they too form a society, a world. Rockwell won't allow us to make light of this. He *never* uses children for superficial sentiment. Indeed, he forbids us to overlook them, as we are wont to do.

This is the nature that grace is given to perfect. Rockwell was a tenuous Christian, and that, rather than his refusal to indulge in filth for filth's sake, marks the limitations of his art. But what he does see, he sees well. To understand why it is not good for the boy and girl to be alone, to understand their toddling steps into the land of marriage, each sex completed by the other, is to begin to understand Catholic social teaching.

4

The Family

Pour out your blessing on us plenteously,
And happy influence upon us rain,
That we may raise a large posterity,
Which from the earth, which they
    may long possess,
With lasting happiness,
Up to your haughty palaces may mount,
And for the guerdon of their glorious merit,
May heavenly tabernacles there inherit,
Of blessed Saints for to increase the count.
—Edmund Spenser, *Epithalamion*, 413-421

And he went down with them, and came to
Nazareth, and was subject unto them: but his
    mother kept all these sayings in her heart.
                    —Luke 2:51

W hen we say that the family is the fundamental natural society, what do we mean? As I've suggested, we are not indulging ourselves in a convenient metaphor. We do not mean that the family *is like a society* or is a society in embryo. It is real and full and holy.

Let art give color and substance to the specters of philosophy. To my mind, Sigrid Undset is the greatest woman novelist who ever lived and is perhaps the only fellow Catholic novelist who can stand the comparison with Alessandro Manzoni. She was a Nobel Laureate and a prolific writer of both fiction and history, including a harrowing piece of autobiography, *Return to the Future*, in which she recounts her escape with one of her two sons from Nazi-invaded Norway to Sweden, to Leningrad, to Moscow, to Vladivostok, to Japan, and finally to San Francisco. The Nazis hated her for her tireless journalistic work against their vicious pagan cult. Undset's other son never left Norway. He died within the first few weeks of battle against the invaders.

Such an impressive woman ought to be celebrated in our universities, but outside of a few Catholic colleges, she is almost wholly ignored. The reason may not be not far to seek. Sigrid Undset began her career as an uneasy feminist, championing the cause of women attempting to make their way in the world of work. Yet she was too fierce a seeker for the truth to remain content with a moral law without a Lawgiver, or economics without households. In an early work, *The Wild Orchid*, she presents us with a fine, strong, independent, secular working mother, whose son Paul eventually rejects her vision of the world and turns instead to Christ. From this point on, Sigrid Undset was *always* writing about households, about strong fathers and strong mothers, or about weakness in the father or the mother, or about how even in the best of marriages the man and the woman are radically incomplete, even for the everyday ordering of their business, without the other.

So Undset committed a cardinal sin. She saw the household, not the workplace, as the heart of life and of true economy. That went along with a greater sin. Brought up to believe in nothing, she converted to the Catholic Faith, affirming that the sanest people she had ever learned about were the saints, oddballs to us, but true men and true women.

Here, at the opening of her masterpiece, *Kristin Lavransdatter*, she introduces us to the heroine's father and mother, shortly after they have been married and have settled on the husband's land:

Lavrans and Ragnfrid were more than commonly pious and God-fearing folk, diligent in church-going, and always pleased to give harbor to God's servants, to messengers sent on the Church's errands, or to pilgrims on their way up the valley to Nidaros; and showing the greatest honor to their parish-priest — who was also their nearest neighbor, living at Rornundgaard. Other folk in the valley were rather given to think that the Church cost them quite dear enough in tithes and in goods and money; and that there was no need to fast and pray so hard besides, or to bring priests and monks into their houses, unless at times when they were really needed. Otherwise the Jorundgaard

folk were much looked up to, and well-liked too; most of
all Lavrans, for he was known as a strong man and a bold,
but peace-loving, quiet and upright, plain in his living but
courteous and seemly in his ways, a rarely good husband-
man and a mighty hunter—'twas wolves and bears and
all kinds of harmful beasts he hunted most keenly. In a
few years he had gotten much land into his hands; but he
was a good and helpful landlord to his tenants.

The household *is a society*. It has its governors, Lavrans and
Ragnfrid. It is related to other households. Lavrans and Ragnfrid have neighbors. They have tenants, whom they treat well.
Lavrans helps to rid the nearby woods of wolves and bears. He
is strong and brave but not given to quarreling. He does not put
on airs; he's a plain dealer. But he's also courteous. He's the sort
of man who would more easily hear a salty story than tell one.
His hard work and his wise use of his resources—cattle, land,
seed, fruit trees, water—help to make him admired and also
give him and Ragnfrid the means to assist the local church and
traveling priests and monks.

Lavrans is not perfect. Wise customs do not require perfection; but they do encourage virtue. He is too mild with his will-
ful daughter, Kristin. He doesn't understand why Ragnfrid is
sometimes dour and reserved and doesn't learn until he is old
that she sometimes needed more passion from him. He is prey
to the ordinary infirmities of human nature, choosing for Kristin
a good man for her to marry, but also the wrong man.

Yet when he lies in bed, dying, we see how a truly Christian
man takes leave of the world. His many friends come to visit
him, one by one, to say goodbye. Last comes his old friend, the
parish priest Sira Eirik, to give him the Sacrament and to pray

with him. Lavrans is awake in his last moments. The priest holds a crucifix before him and begs him to look upon his Savior as they utter together the words of Christ upon the Cross: *In manus tuas spiritum meum commendo.*

A far cry from the loneliness and terrible triviality of a modern death, in a hospital, with the television droning and the beep, beep of the intravenous machine continuing to let no one in particular know that it is still doing its work, although it is now in vain. But then, what we have in the household is a human *reality*, not a mechanism like the modern hospital, or an abstraction like the modern State.

When we turn away from abstractions to human realities, much of our confusion clears away. "Patriarchy," for example, is an abstraction, used to frighten or appall; but a father is not an abstraction. A father is a man. And once we admit the obvious, that husbands and wives make households, and that a child ought to have a father and a mother, and that it's the man who is the father and the woman who is the mother, then much of what some people consider scandalous follows as a matter of course and feels, for ordinary people, as natural as the sun rising in the east.

The Pope and the Papa

If the family is a society, how is it governed?

The same St. Paul who says, in several places, that God is not a respecter of persons, advises the early Christians to "be subject to higher powers" (cf. Rom. 13:1) and exhorts them to be a body built up of mutual love and obedience. For all authority comes from God. Therefore, as Leo writes in *Immortale Dei*, "to despise legitimate authority, in whomsoever vested, is unlawful, as a rebellion against the divine will" (110). That does not mean that all Christian societies must be monarchies. It does mean that, even in democracies, justice does not arise from the consent of the governed, since that would deny the participation of human law in the divine law. If "government is nothing more nor less than the will of the people, and the people, being under the power of itself alone, is alone its own ruler," then "the authority of God is passed over in silence," and "a State becomes nothing but a multitude" (*ID*, 120).

Granted that law and authority are of divine origin, there can be no true human society without the virtue of obedience. This virtue is not the same as compelled concession, any more than authority is the same as coercion. Our nation sags under innumerable laws whose origin and content no one knows, so that we can hardly take a step without violating nine or ten of them; we comply with these laws, perhaps, but we do not obey them. *We do not heed them*; we do not take their lawfulness into our hearts. We do not assume, in our persons, by our obedience, the rightful authority of those who have given us the laws. And because we must comply with other men—or, worse, with the vast machinery of government that no one can any longer describe or control—rather than obey God and His designated subordinates, we do not enjoy genuine social liberty; and because the machine rewards the moral squalor on which it feeds, we must enact our compliance while bound in chains.

It is in this context that we must see Pope Leo's affirmation of patriarchal authority. "A family," he writes in *Rerum novarum*, "no less than a State, is, as we have said, a true society, governed by a power within its sphere, that is to say, by the father" (215). At the time of the encyclical (1891), this was probably the *least controversial* thing he had to say. Of course he has plenty of scriptural warrant. St. Peter advises his flock, "Submit yourselves to every ordinance of man for the Lord's sake" (1 Pet. 2:13), and from there he proceeds to outline the duties of all Christians toward one another, not as indifferent individuals, but as members of a body with particular duties. "Wives, be in subjection to your own husbands," he says (1 Pet. 3:1), even husbands who are unbelievers, that they may be brought around, and husbands are to cherish their wives and to honor them as "being heirs together of the grace of life; that your prayers be not hindered" (1 Pet. 3:7). Without such authority and obedience, the command that sums up the Christian social and ecclesial life would be impossible: "Finally, be ye all of one mind" (1 Pet. 3:8).

As Leo makes clear, this authority does not derive from human custom or consent. It is the principal reason the State may not usurp the rights of the family: "Paternal authority can neither be abolished nor absorbed by the State; for it has the same source as human life itself" (*RN*, 215). In other words, the authority of the father in the home derives from the Fatherhood of God. That does not mean that human fathers are better or smarter than human mothers, any more than it means that a priest must be holier than a parishioner, or a head must be healthier than a hand. It does, however, suggest why the decline of fatherhood in the home is promoted by those who wish to enlarge the State.

It also means that the father may not do as he pleases. His fatherhood is not primary, but contingent; it is conferred upon him by the Father. So Leo notes that among the ancient Romans arose the complementary evils of State control of marriage, such that "permission to marry, or the refusal of the permission, depended upon the will of the heads of State" (*AD*, 61); and the custom of easy divorce, allowing the man to assume "right of dominion over his wife," and, as St. Jerome said, "to run headlong with impunity into lust." The result combined an arrogant

State with a debased and debauched family life: "Of necessity the offspring of such marriages as these were either reckoned among the stock in trade of the commonwealth or held to be the property of the father of the family; and the law permitted him to make and unmake the marriages of his children at his mere will, and even to exercise against them the monstrous power of life and death" (*AD*, 62).

These things, then, imply one another. The true society is bound by law and obedience, not by human statutes and compliance. Law derives its obligatory nature not from contractual utility, but from its participation in divine law. That participation requires a recognized authority, not the competition of individual wills. The Church is a society — indeed, notwithstanding all the sins of her members, the most perfect society we will ever see on earth. The family is a society. The family, then, requires law, which other societies must respect, because otherwise they would contradict their own being. God is the source of all authority on earth. Indeed, says Leo in *Diuturnum*, "the authority of fathers of families preserves a certain impressed image and form of the authority which is of God, 'of whom all paternity in heaven and earth is named'" (143; cf. Eph. 3:15). With that authority come grave duties. For one, fathers must never entrust their children to sources of corruption in schools. They must come together, says Leo, with other fathers to see to it that their children are raised with firm morals, knowledge of religion, and piety toward God, and that it is damnable in them "should they commit children at a credulous and incautious age to the hazard of untrustworthy teachers" (*Officio sanctissimo* [Letter to the bishops of Bavaria, December 22, 1887], 2402; translation mine).

Now, then, if you wish to destroy a society and reduce it to a compliant although vicious rabble, or if you wish, as we will see,

to destroy the society of the Church and reduce it to a conge-
ries of self-willed parishes, themselves divided into factions and
cliques and atomized individuals all going their own way, here
are some obvious things to do.

Get the father out of the family, leaving it prey to the ministrations of the State. Get the father out of the Church, leaving
it prey to the vagaries of popular taste. Get the Father out of the
Bible, emptying the faith and turning Christ Himself into a fool
or a liar. Then you will have in the family, in the State, and in
the Church not law but the exercise of raw will.

The Family and Education

Now comes a predictable objection. "We used to need such
families as you describe, but economic conditions are different
now, and the family has shrunk accordingly. People no longer
run shops out of their homes or live off the land. A single parent
will do now."

There are plenty of studies that show that single parents will
not do even for the small range of human goods that are count-
able, but that's not to the point. As always we return to first principles. The family is not the creation of the State. It is also not
the result of mere material circumstances. The *accidents* of family
life are. So the members of a family will wear one sort of cloth-
ing or eat one sort of food or maintain one set of daily chores
rather than others, depending on whether they herd sheep near
the desert or hunker down in igloos for the winter. That is not
in dispute. But *what a family is*, essentially, does not change, and
cannot change, because the way children are conceived and born
does not change. Just as the human person is a composite of body
and soul, so the human family is both natural and directed by
and toward what transcends the natural.

The Family

To make one's definition of the family depend upon mass economics is thus to get things backward. The family is not for economics. Economics are for the family. Suppose all our material needs are met, and we do not have to bother with purchase and trade. Would that mean we would have no households, no law, no family? Are we parents and children only when we sweat?

Obviously not, because we are not made for work. The week is not an interminable series of Mondays. It is meant to be steeped in the joy and the rest and the celebration of the Sabbath past and the Sabbath to come. This is another way of saying that man is most human when, like the genial poet Hopkins, he looks up at the "fire-folk" in the heavens—the stars. Food is good and for the health of the body. Truth, beauty, and goodness are sweeter, and they are for the health of the soul. Parents are to raise children sound in both body and soul. *Their prime duty, after working for one another's salvation, is to teach their children what will avail them in this world and in the next.*

This duty, which is also a right because it is a duty, was never far from Leo's mind when he wrote about the family and the rights of even the poorest among us. He understood that the secularists of his day sought to destroy the Faith by capturing the minds of children. But "the training of youth most conducive to the defense of true faith and religion and to the preservation of morality," he writes in his inaugural letter, "must find its beginning from an early stage within the circle of home life" (*I*, 17). The duty of parents is a facet of the blessed order of the family society: "Parents are bound to give all care and watchful thought to the education of their offspring and their virtuous bringing up: *Fathers, . . . bring them up* [that is, your children] *in the discipline and correction of the Lord* (*AD*, 65; emphasis in the original; cf. Eph. 6:4). The indissolubility of marriage helps "to secure the holy education of children" (*AD*, 72). Even in Catholic high schools, says Leo, the "rights of parents claim respect and protection" (*Militantis Ecclesia* [1897], 1320; translation mine).

We may be too generous if we believe that our enemies disagree with us on how to *assist* families. The most honest of them openly seek to encroach upon the family and render it inconsequential. To corrupt family life — literally, to break down the household, the domestic society, *corrumpere societatem domesticam* — they must inflict "cruel outrage," *iniuria*, on the parents (*SC*, 206). We see this sort of thing all the time, and in ways that Leo himself could not have believed possible, boys and girls instructed in "safe" fornication and sexual deviance without even the notification of their parents, much less their approval. But parents "hold from nature their right of training the children to whom they have given birth, with the obligation superadded of shaping and directing the education of their little ones to the end for which God vouchsafed the privilege of transmitting the gift of life." Parents must "strain every nerve" to ward off the invasion, and "strive manfully to have and to hold exclusive authority to direct the education of their offspring, as is fitting." It is a "great and pernicious error" to contend that "the civil government should at its option intrude into and exercise intimate control over the family and the household" (*RN*, 215). It is also pernicious to remove from the family the capacity to educate their children in religiously oriented schools, as the French government did, "bringing immeasurable harm to the faith of the coming generation, despite the protests of the entire episcopate and of the fathers of families" (*Les Evenements* [Letter to the President of France, May 12, 1883], 2591; translation mine).

Leo never changed his mind about this. In his silver jubilee review of his pontificate, *Pervenuti all'anno* (1903), he decries the foolish ambitions of those who would absorb the family into the State. For the State, "forgetting its limitations and the essential object of the authority which it wields, has laid its hands on the marriage bond to profane it and has stripped it of its religious character; it has dared as much as it could in the matter of that natural right which parents possess to educate their children, and in many countries it has destroyed the stability of marriage by giving a legal sanction to the licentious institution of divorce" (PAA, 561-562). *Malnata licenzia*: that's what Leo calls it; *license born in evil hour.*

We see that the three moves of the State reinforce one another. Marriage must be secularized, if divorce is to become common; and if divorce is common, or even if we accept that marriage is not in principle perpetual, then *of course* the education of children cannot be entrusted to a transient mother or a transient father. The child will have been torn from, or deprived of, the human history into which he was born; and the State intrudes to fill up the vacuity with slogans and servitude. So it is that the officials in charge of education in one Canadian province have recently declared themselves to be "co-parents," thus reducing man to a creature of the State, rather than seeing the State as the creation of families.

Pope Leo thus approves heartily of the equity of laws then current in the United States, which allowed for the free and energetic creation of "unnumbered religious and useful institutions, sacred edifices, schools for the instruction of youth," and colleges, hospitals, convents, and monasteries (*Longinquae oceani*, 323). The words that are translated as "schools," *ludos litterarios*, suggest that the main purpose of education is literary in the broad sense, to introduce young people to works that form the imagination and move their hearts and minds to love the truth.

Such education as Leo had in mind has almost vanished even from parochial schools. But "the more the enemies of religion exert themselves to offer the uninformed, especially the young, such instruction as darkens the mind and corrupts morals," he writes, "the more actively should we endeavor that not only a suitable and solid method of education may flourish" (*I*, 17).

That solid education would be founded in philosophy, which for Leo was the realism of Thomas Aquinas, for philosophy, unlike the secular enemies, "seeks not the overthrow of divine revelation, but delights rather to prepare its way, and defend it against assailants" (*I*, 17). It must also direct the mind and heart toward God. Hence, Leo abominates as an offense to God and man the Naturalist's opinion that "in the education of youth nothing is to be taught in the matter of religion as of certain and fixed opinion" (*HG*, 95). The child learns not so much that God is too great for the school, but that He is too small. They fall prone to the "absurd theories of Idealism, or the most abject theories of Materialism" (*Officio sanctissimo*, 2394; translation mine). It is a "godless education of youth" (*ID*, 122). A truly Christian people would make public provision "for the instruction of youth in religion and true morality" (*ID*, 130). Instead, religion is ignored in school when the children are small and then undermined when they are older, by "evil teaching," for example, "that matter alone exists in the world; that men and beasts have the same origin and a like nature" (*EIA*, 167). The enemies "are in possession of numerous schools, taken by violence from the Church, in which, by ridicule and scurrilous jesting, they pervert the credulous and unformed minds of the young, to the contempt of Holy Scripture" (*Providentissimus Deus*, 282).

If *truth* is our guide, then what Leo criticizes as the "liberty of teaching" needs also to be properly understood. It is one thing if we mean liberty to search for truths we do not possess. It is another if we mean liberty to speak against the truth. That is license, and "license will gain what liberty loses" (*PD*, 152), and will "pervert men's minds," turning the teacher's office "with impunity into an instrument of corruption" (*PD*, 153). Evil teachings poison the mind, and "the moral character becomes at the same time deeply and substantially corrupt" (*EIA*, 167), for no one will "be inclined to do right who has been accustomed to make self-love the sole rule of what he should do or avoid doing" (*EIA*, 171).

What's a Family For?

We should not, however, give the impression that the prime function of a family is the godly education of children. We should not locate the good of a family in any *function* at all. The question is miscast. A family is not for a *what*, but for *persons*, and for God.

Recall what a person is. A dog is born in time, but not in history. The child is born already within a matrix of relationships that extend far backward in time and that can be expected to extend far forward. He has grandparents and great-grandparents, aunts and uncles, first cousins and more distant kinsmen whose number is hard to determine. He may well marry and have children and grandchildren of his own.

A dog may have a pedigree, but it means nothing to the dog. The child without relations — without the history of blood itself — feels deprived of something central to his humanity. That history gives him a human place and all the duties of piety that belong to that place. The ancient Romans, as Leo well knew, grew up under the very gaze of those who had gone before them. Their departed kin, in plaster masks made upon their death, or in figurines, looked upon them from the mantel over the hearth. They became tutelary deities of the family, the clan — the household gods. They were false gods, no doubt, but they did adumbrate something of the truth. For our capacity to recall, to memorialize, to make the past present and to take action for the future, seeing the future in the seed now and in the past, suggests that we do not live as mere subjects of time, as the other creatures on earth do.

In the family, *through* the temporal relations of the family, the child learns indeed that he is oriented beyond time, to God. He is not an animal but an immortal creature. By the very existence of such a thing as the family, he learns in the pulses of his blood that he is not an atom colliding against other atoms in empty and meaningless space. He learns that he is from and with and for others; and in a Christian family he learns that he is from God, for God, with God as his Shepherd. In the family, he learns not to eat like a dog, but to share a meal, like a human being; he learns to celebrate, to worship. In the Christian family, he learns to long for "the one thing which is necessary, viz.: that ultimate good for which we are all born into the world" (*Graves de communi*, 485).

If we are talking, then, about Catholic social teaching, but not about what a family is, and the transcendent goods toward which it directs the hearts of both parents and children, then we are talking about a contradiction in terms — an economy without households, a society without friendship. To pretend that we can do without the family is as absurd as to pretend that we can do without friendship, humanity, and the Author of both, the God who stole into human history in the form of a little child, in Bethlehem, two thousand years ago.

5

Social Life

*Every man in our village had been helping for months
in the evenings to build our chapel. I used to play in the
bricks and blocks and plaster with the other boys while the
men were working, and fine times we did have. Indeed,
the Chapel looks the same now as the day it was opened
by some preacher from Town. We had no preacher of
our own for a long time because the village was not rich
enough to pay one, so the grown-ups took turns to preach
and pray, and of course the choir was always there.*
—Richard Llewellyn, *How Green Was My Valley*

*I am glad of the coming of Stephanas and Fortunatus and
Achaicus: for that which was lacking on your part they
have supplied. For they have refreshed my spirit and yours:
therefore acknowledge ye them that are such. The churches
of Asia salute you. Aquila and Priscilla salute you much
in the Lord, with the church that is in their house. All the
brethren greet you. Greet ye one another with an holy
kiss. The salutation of me Paul with mine own hand.*
—1 Corinthians 16:17-21

When Alexis de Tocqueville visited the United States in the early nineteenth century, what struck him most powerfully was the American penchant for association. Things had not yet been reduced to the State and the individual, the former a monstrous abstraction, the latter a cripple. Everywhere he turned, he met free associations of people uniting to attain some good, which was usually *not merely private to the club.*

I am thumbing through a selection of Abraham Lincoln's addresses. Here is one before the Young Men's Lyceum of Springfield, Illinois, a debating and educational society, on the proposed subject "The perpetuation of our political institutions." Here is another before the Springfield Washingtonian Temperance Society, a group of former alcoholics, on sincere friendship as the best strategy for winning men over to the cause. I find one on the value of labor, and the mobility it can bring, before the Wisconsin State Agricultural Society, in Milwaukee. Here is his famous address on slavery at the educational and social Cooper Institute, in New York City.

It's hard for us to imagine how thoroughly *social* human life was in the free United States, before the advent of mass entertainment, mass schooling, mass administration, mass production of goods, mass marketing, and mass politics. Long before schooling was made compulsory, one could rely on the literacy of every adult of sound mind in such states as Massachusetts, Pennsylvania, and New York. Everyone *built things*, and they could do that only by working together. A handful of farmers and artisans would set about, as soon as they were able, to build a church and hire a preacher. Then they would build a school, appoint a school board, and hire a schoolteacher. They would build their own local roads and maintain them. When their numbers grew large enough, they would petition the state to incorporate as a town or borough. They would build their town hall, with their own hands. They would pass town ordinances, without looking over their shoulders at the state capital or at Washington.

They had community songfests, church socials, barn raisings, dances, debate clubs, fairs, spelling bees, quilting bees, and concerts. They came together to saw ice from frozen ponds, to bank their rivers with levees, and to clear forests for the railroad. They had town ball clubs and opera houses. They had beneficent societies for the poor. Members of fraternities pooled their resources for the succor of widows and orphans. They built hospitals. They built high schools and colleges. They sang together, marched together in parades, prayed together, played together, brawled in saloons together, fought against one another and beside one another, hated one another, loved one another, mourned the neighbor's passing away, rejoiced for the neighbor's newborn child; they knew one another's names, and the names of their brothers and sisters, parents and grandparents and cousins. They were not saints. They were only human beings, but they *were* human beings, not atoms in an amorphous mass, and not apiary units in a hive. They were social.

Social, Not Socialist

Pope Leo therefore sees *both* the adulation of the self *and* the arrogance of the State as enemies to a truly healthy and dynamic society; and he sees them as springing from the same source, for neither one will acknowledge in man the natural duties that he owes to God, his family, his neighbors and fellow workers, and his countrymen, natural duties that imply rights to fulfill them and restrictions against State encroachment, usurpation, or dissolution. Jesus did not command us to love "mankind." There is no such reductive abstraction in true Christian morality. Jesus commanded us to love God with all our heart and soul and mind and strength, and to love our *neighbor* as ourselves. The neighbor is not someone conveniently on the other side of the world. The neighbor is inconveniently here, now. He is the man who never mows his lawn and who drinks too much. She is the woman escaping from her troubled home to meddle in the lives of the victims of her benevolence. He is the man fallen among thieves, right there in the ditch, bleeding his life away.

This love of neighbor extends to a perfectly proper love of country and submission to its laws and its lawgivers. Thus, Leo condemns "that sect of men who, under the motley and all but barbarous terms and titles of socialists, communists, and nihilists, are spread abroad throughout the world," in alliance "to carry out the purpose long resolved upon, of uprooting the foundations of civil society at large" (QAM, 22). Leo admits that not every man who calls himself a socialist understands the great aim of his society aimed at dissolving society. But it all springs from a kind of socialized or organized hatred of the social.

Let me explain. To attack the right of private property is to attack man as a time-transcending being, who works the land his father worked and passes it on to his children. To attack the family is to attack man at the heart of both his material and his spiritual nature, severing him from the love and the duty of his very blood. To attack or dismiss the Church is to bend man's neck under the yoke of materialism and cast his gaze to the earth—not to the graves where his forebears rest, but to perishable stuff, so that man will esteem himself not according to what he is, but according to what he has, or rather what someone else has that he does not have.

The socialists go farther than this; they must go farther. The nation itself, a man's *country*, must in effect be abolished. "The old land of my fathers is beloved to me," begins the Welsh national anthem. "I love thy rocks and rills, thy woods and templed hills," sang Americans, back in the day when they did sing and did love the boulders and creeks of their native land. It is a personal, human relationship. Seacoasts, mountains, rocks, and pools are not the objects of abstract political programs. The orioles that herald the fullness of spring obey their nature and not an ideology.

These things are not chosen by man. They are given to him, and they claim his allegiance and love. But the socialist must demote them or deny them. Hence, says Leo, "the hallowed dignity and authority of rulers has incurred much odium on the part of rebellious subjects that evil-minded traitors, spurning all control, have many a time within a recent period boldly raised impious hands against the very heads of States" (QAM, 23). Such men are "disloyal"—Latin *perfidi*, of twisted or perverted faith. They threaten "the civilized community" itself.

Notice what Leo recommends here. It is not simply that we comply with the wishes of authorities. It is rather piety itself. Just as we do not choose our parents, so we do not choose our kings, and even in democracies we choose only the people who will administer the government and the land handed on to us by our forebears; although it may well be that the rage of the mass of men to choose, or of some few ambitious men to be chosen by the masses, makes for dissatisfaction all around, as we choose scoundrels and then despise the scoundrels we so habitually choose. That is a far cry from the reverence that Pope Leo says we owe to legitimate rulers. But reverence, like filial piety, patriotism, and devotion to God, is necessarily and ardently personal. It is never the object of a humanitarian program.

So if we want a just society, or any society at all, we must promote what is social. We must promote the fundamental virtue of piety.

Again, we see that the wellspring of society is the home. In the domestic circle fashioned by Christian life, says Pope Leo, men and women grow to love religion and abhor impiety, and to pursue that difficult goal, virtue, "to the restraint of that insatiable seeking after self-interest alone, which so spoils and *weakens* the character of men" (*I*, 18; emphasis mine). The verb he uses is *enervat*: it literally tears the sinews out. Virtue—manliness, in its ancient sense—requires a muscular character. How does one build up the musculature of the spirit? What will give strength to well-raised children when they go forth from the home into the greater world? Leo turns to "those pious associations which have been established ... with so great profit to the cause of the Catholic religion" (*I*, 19).

We find this recommendation again and again in the Pope's letters. He sees, parading under the name of socialism, the destruction of the social, and, parading under the name of liberalism (which might now be called Conservatism in some quarters), the destruction of liberty. Therefore, he looks to free associations of men and women. For the encouragement and the support of Christian family life, he turns to those pious societies that in his day were the muscles of a Catholic parish. We still retain a few of these here and there: the Holy Name Society, the

Altar and Rosary Society. Most of them, however, were washed away in the name of progress, and their place remembers them no more.

These small societies were both supernatural (they were watered by the grace of God and were directed toward worship) and natural (they helped to fulfill the longing of the human person for friendship, with both God and man). We will find this double orientation too throughout Leo's letters. It is why, for example, in *Aeterni Patris* he urges all bishops to set the work of St. Thomas Aquinas at the center of a seminarian's education. We might well sum it up in Thomas's dictum that grace perfects nature and consider that the whole of Catholic social teaching is rooted in that relationship. It is grace and grace alone that perfects nature, so that a radically secular society—or radically secular agencies for the amelioration of some social ill—must fail, just as a plant must wither and die when you pull it up by its roots. Catholic social teaching requires a vigorous relationship between civic life and the Church, lest civic life itself grow diseased and die.

For example, let us suppose that working men suffer under the impersonality or the callous cruelty of "capital," of owners who have themselves never gone down a mine, or pulled a barge along a river, or hauled on their shoulders bags of seed weighing over a hundred pounds. These laborers are easy marks for the socialists: "Wearied out by sheer hard work, [they] are more easily entrapped by the hope of wealth and the promise of prosperity" (QAM, 32-33), a hope that Leo sees is usually delusive, for the demagogues, for their own ambitions, cause the people to believe they can enjoy wealth without labor and virtue, and "their lying promises will only one day bring forth evils worse than the present" (*RN*, 218). Therefore, "it seems expedient

to encourage associations"—Latin *societates*, societies, friendships—"for handicraftsmen and laboring men, which, placed
under the sheltering care of religion, may render the members
content with their lot and resigned to toil, inducing them to
lead a peaceful and tranquil life" (QAM, 33).

We must not think that he is recommending mere resigna-
tion. It requires strength to live modestly and decently. And
that strength comes not from within the individual. It comes
from God, mediated through the Church and through other
human beings, in capacities both natural and supernatural. So,
against the depredations of the clandestine Freemasons and other
secularists, Pope Leo recommends "that the Third Order of St.
Francis, whose discipline We a little while ago prudently miti-
gated," evidently with the merciful aim to extend its goodness as
widely as possible, "should be studiously promoted and sustained:
for the whole object of this Order, as constituted by its founder,
is to invite men to an imitation of Jesus Christ, to a love of the
Church, and to the observance of all Christian virtues," so that
the minds of men will be drawn "to liberty, fraternity, and equality of right," the liberty that "Jesus Christ obtained for the human
race and St. Francis aspired to: the liberty, We mean, of *sons of
God*, through which we may be free from slavery to Satan or to
our passions"—Latin *cupiditatibus*, lusts—"both of them most
wicked masters" (HG, 103).

And he also recommends what we somewhat inaccurately
might call unions, "the associations or guilds," *scholas seu col-
legia*, schools or colleges, that is, institutions of apprenticeship
and camaraderie, "of workmen, for the protection, under the
guidance of religion, both of their temporal interests and of their
morality" (HG, 103). I will return to the guilds more specifically
in a later chapter. I wish to stress here that the good of the guild

or sodality is, for Leo, not occasional. It does not depend upon circumstances. For "it cannot be doubted but that by the will of God, men are united in civil society; whether its component parts be considered; or its form, which implies authority; or the object of its existence; or the abundance of the vast services which it renders to man" (*LP*, 150). God Himself has made man to be social.

When human beings do unite to form these associations, they are exercising a natural right, in the service of a natural duty, to seek the common good. Therefore the associations, says Pope Leo, "possess the sanction of the law of nature" (*RN*, 241). Insofar as they are religious associations, "the rulers of the State accordingly have no rights over them, nor can they claim any share in their control; on the contrary, it is the duty of the State to respect and cherish them, and, if need be, to defend them from attack." It is not just that a Henry VIII had no right to smother the life of English villages by plundering the abbeys, priories, church schools, convents, and hospitals upon which the common people, especially the poor, depended. It is also beyond the legitimate power of the State to control them, let us say by requiring the Little Sisters of the Poor to put money in the collection basket for contraceptives and abortifacients. This point requires some further explanation. We must return to the meaning of a body.

The Body and Its Parts

It may sound odd to our ears, that socialists, whose prescriptions for society are many and comprehensive, should be united with nihilists, who by definition believe in nothing. But Pope Leo, beginning as always from a rich view of human nature grounded in reason and elevated by revelation, sees the alliance we miss — and by implication he includes as well the fellow traveler, secular liberalism, friendlier to the free market but ultimately also an enemy to man.

How so? Let us focus on two of the evils Leo discusses in his letter *Quod apostolici muneris*. The first is the denial of the body; the second, the severance of human law from divine law, effacing in citizens the sense of moral obligation or piety. We obey such human laws because it is to our advantage, narrowly and materially conceived, to do so, not because it is right and just.

Human beings do not have bodies as a plumber has a wrench or a doctor has a probe. Nor are they bodies, simply, reducible to their constituent parts; even a dog is more than the sum of its parts. Human beings are embodied rational souls, and everything they touch they mark with the fire of their spirit, the gift of God. That is the ground of their right to property. But they are not solitary atoms either, rebounding against one another in a chaotic war of all against all. For the human soul is made for love and can attain its end only by communion with other souls. Therefore, long before we meet the State, we find human beings fashioning not artificial but real bodies in turn: families and clans and villages.

It is absolutely crucial to understand this. Catholic social teaching affirms the reality of the bodies that human beings form; they are not notional, but real and living, and they imply real rights and duties among the members, who are themselves not mere parts, but whole persons. The touchstone is the Church herself, wherein God has "established different grades of orders with diversity of functions, so that all should not be apostles, all not doctors, all not prophets" (cf. 1 Cor. 12:28-29). The State, "like the Church, should form one body comprising many members, some excelling others in rank and importance, but all alike necessary to one another and solicitous for the common welfare"

(*QAM*, 27). This is not the Leviathan that Thomas Hobbes imagined. It is not the result of a "social contract" that intrinsically solitary men (Leo's astute word is *solivagum, wandering alone*) create for their individual purposes, for that is *commentitium et fictum*, a deception and a fiction, lacking the strength, the dignity, the stability, and the security that a genuine republic requires (*Diuturnum*, 146). No one loves a contract.

We learn solicitude for the common welfare not from the State, however, but within the fostering home of the Church and the family. The family circle, says the Pope, is "the starting-point of every city and every state," resting upon "the indissoluble union of husband and wife" (*QAM*, 27). Leo makes the connections we miss, because we have lost his strong sense of human bodily realities. All living bodies require order; that is the basis of St. Paul's warning to the Corinthians. Not all can be teachers or prophets or priests. The hand cannot see; the eye cannot grasp. But the enemies of these bodies cry up an equality that is wholly abstract—mathematical, even mechanical. Says the Pope, they "contend that all men are by nature equal, and hence they contend that neither honor nor respect is owed to public authority, nor any obedience to the laws, saving perhaps to those which have been sanctioned according to their good pleasure" (*QAM*, 26).

Absurd? Doesn't our Declaration of Independence declare that all men are created equal? The crucial word, though, is *created*. The equality—even in the mind of the deist Jefferson—is an endowment by God. Leo explains what it really means: "From the Gospel records, equality among men consists in this, that one and all, possessing the same nature, are called to the sublime dignity of being sons of God; and, moreover, that one and the same end being set before all, each and every one has to be judged according to the same laws" (QAM, 26). We are equal in our nature and, to say the same thing in another way, in the goal toward which we naturally tend. Hence Leo, in his encyclical *In Plurimis* (1888), addressed to Brazilian bishops on the abolition of slavery *de iure* and *de facto*, cites with approval this brave passage from the early Church Father Lactantius: "Should anyone say: Are there not among you some poor, some rich, some slaves, some who are masters; is there no difference between different persons? I answer: There is none, nor is there any other cause why we call each other by the name of brother than that we consider ourselves to be equals; for, when we measure all human things, *not by the body but by the spirit*, although their corporal condition may be different from ours, yet in spirit they are not slaves to us, but we esteem and call them brethren, fellow workers in religion" (302; cf. *Divine Institutes*, 5.16). "Do not, then, call any Christian man a slave," says Leo, in abhorrence of any such antisocial institution, "unless, indeed, he is in bondage again to sin" (301).

But when people no longer recognize their divine source and end, and forget the genuine spiritual equality that subsists among them, they substitute for it an artificial equality in goods, violating the rights, Pope Leo says, of private property, claiming "that all may with impunity seize upon the possessions and usurp the rights of the wealthy" (QAM, 30). In other words, they seek equality where it is not to be had and destroy the inequality — we may say, diversity — that God has ordained: "More wisely and profitably the Church recognizes the existence of inequality among men, who are by nature unlike in mental endowment and strength of body, and even in amount of fortune." Therefore the Church enjoins that "the right of property and of its disposal, derived from nature, should in the case of every individual remain intact and inviolate."

The poor, then, are out of luck? No. We must clear away the weeds of wrong thinking. We must cease conceiving of "the rich" and "the poor" as abstractions, or as nameless masses, or as parts of a national machine. A society can only be a society of persons, with the rights and duties that flow from their God-given nature as persons meant to be bound in love. The Church, says Leo, is a loving mother—he is not using a metaphor here—and addresses in her motherly care both those who are rich and those who are poor.

She holds that the poor "represent the person of Christ Himself," and so she "brings them aid to the utmost of her power, takes thought to have erected in every land in their behoof homes and refuges where they can be received, nurtured, and tended" (QAM, 30-31). He is describing here the care of persons, not numbers; a care that can be given only in love and that binds in a relationship of loyalty and gratitude both him who gives and him who receives. But love is also our duty, so the Church "lays the rich under strict command to give of their superfluity to the poor, impressing them with fear of the divine judgment which will exact the penalty of eternal punishment unless they succor the wants of the needy."

May that be done by confiscatory taxes? Not even by modest taxes. The obligation is personal. I am not saying, nor is Leo saying, that taxes may never be levied for the alleviation of need. But such taxation, even if it were necessary, would not be sufficient. And here we touch upon the great error of the modern State, which Leo sees quite clearly. It is that "governments have been organized without God and the order established by Him being taken at all into account," something even the pagans never did. The Church has been forced to withdraw from "the scheme of studies at universities, colleges, and high schools, as well as from all the practical working of public life" (QAM, 24). That severs our public life from the life to come and removes at a stroke the profound and personal obligations, God-given along with our rights, which the rich and poor owe to one another. A Scrooge can thus say that he "gives" to the poor because he is taxed to support poorhouses and orphanages; and our modern statists can say that because they tax others to support a wholly dysfunctional way of life, they therefore have given to the poor.

We are forbidden to steal, says Leo. We are forbidden even to covet. Why is that? Why does the commandment reach down into the depths of the heart? A cog in a machine cannot covet. If an atom in the great impersonal materialist modern State covets, what harm, so long as the State can make him keep his hands to himself? But here we see the strange harmony between one form of worldly covetousness and another—the form that sees the amassing of private fortune as the *summum bonum*, and the form that believes in a mechanical and mathematical redistribution, without regard to the human person. Catholic social teaching sees both forms of materialism as evil from the root.

When God rained manna upon the Israelites in the desert, they were forbidden to hoard it. They were forbidden to treat it as quantity, rather than as a gift from a personal God to persons made in His image. When they tried to do so anyway, the manna rotted and stank. It is high time we ceased thinking of masses and quantity and remembered duty and love. That should strike all of us, rich and poor alike, with trembling.

Church Societies

It may seem strange that organizations of Christians united to teach children, assist the poor, give homes to orphans, heal the sick, and comfort the dying have long been in the gun sights of "enlightened" thinkers in the West. Supporters of the so-called right to dispose of one's unborn child do not actually want Christians to give more and more assistance to unwed mothers; secular leaders in mass education do not actually wish there were more and more Christian schools, embarrassingly successful as they are, in our decadent cities; apostate members of Catholic religious orders who continue to work within the Church they hate are not actually pleased to see the resurgence of new, vibrant, orthodox orders, filled with young people eager to evangelize a sad and silly world. The heart of an academic feminist would sink to hear that men of old may have loved their wives and been not nearly so domineering as she, nursing her enmity and envious of women who manage to get along with men naturally and happily, has wanted so desperately to believe. The mass educators avert their eyes, lest they see bright, happy, and truly social children graduating from schools whose old-fashioned piety those educators scorn. And as for the apostates, they, the nerves of their souls so pitilessly exposed to every hair's touch of meekness, every breath of innocent devotion, need the most careful spiritual care to be brought back to health; for it must be agony to them to be in the presence of young and cheerful nuns and priests who love the Church.

Strange it may seem, but it is true. No longer think of man as man, made by God and for God, and he becomes instead a thing, either to promote some supposedly ideal state of affairs, or to clear out of its way. Hence, like Auguste Comte, you may come to hate the Church's beneficent societies and wish their destruction, precisely because they do help the poor, and that makes the poor less likely to do your bidding and rise up in revolt.

So Pope Leo had often to defend not only the record of the great religious orders, but their very existence. That is the subject of his letter to the religious congregations in France, on December 23, 1900, *Au milieu des consolations*. "We have been struck with sadness," he writes, "at the news of the dangers which threaten the religious congregations in France. By dint of misunderstanding and prejudice it has come to be thought that it will be necessary for the good of the State to put restraints upon their liberty, and perhaps to proceed against them with even greater rigor" (AMC, 495).

The religious orders are a standing reproach to the ambition and the spiritual weakness of the secular State. The object of the consecrated life, says Leo, is twofold: "First, the raising of those who take [vows] to a higher degree of perfection; and secondly, by purifying and strengthening their souls, to prepare them for a ministry which is exercised for the salvation of their neighbor and for the alleviation of the numberless miseries of humanity" (AMC, 496). The consecrated life is profoundly personal and freely admits of inequality, of degrees of perfection. Its prime purpose is union with God and, through that ever-deepening personal relationship, a deepening friendship with one's neighbor, for his *salut*—his salvation, but also his well-being generally, his health in body and soul. And these are things that the secular State cannot achieve. It does not build societies; it manages masses of men for the sake of some material goal.

See, however, what the religious orders have done. They have, first, taught everyone who was capable of hearing, "preaching virtue to the multitude by the apostolate of good example," and "forming and adorning men's minds by the teaching of sacred and profane knowledge," and "enlarging the heritage of the fine arts by splendid works that will live" (AMC, 497). That is, the Church has brought beauty, both within the minds of men—Leo's word is *embellir*, embellishing, beautifying, adorning—and to their eyes and minds, by means of the patrimony *des beaux artes*, the beautiful arts. Such things are not for individuals alone, those cripples, but for men: and so Leo will continually defend the Church as the great social promoter of the arts and of human learning generally.

But the religious orders did not merely confer benefits upon existing societies. They were societies that *created societies*. This is a plain historical fact. Here let me quote Pope Leo in full, as he describes the creation of a new Europe from the ashes of the Roman Empire and the devastation wrought by the pagan barbarians:

> Whilst their doctors shed renown on the universities by the depth and breadth of their learning, and their houses became the refuge of divine and human knowledge, and in the shipwreck of civilization saved from certain destruction the masterpieces of ancient wisdom, other religious have penetrated inhospitable regions, swamps or tangled forests, and there, braving every danger in draining and clearing and cultivating the land by the sweat of their brow, they founded round their monasteries and beneath the shadow of the cross centers of population which grew into villages and flourishing towns, whence, under a kindly rule, agriculture and industry began to spread abroad.

Here we may think of the bold young Bernard of Clairvaux, of a rather frail constitution, who nevertheless went forth into the German wilderness with a small group of Cistercian monks to found a new monastery; for Germany became arable only under the picks and spades of Christian monks working and praying to the glory of God.

But that, although great, was not all. What does it profit a man if he build a town, but his townsmen lead vicious lives and lose their souls? So the same religious orders that created societies brought additional benefits to the societies growing up around them. They gave them a spiritual orientation; which is another way of saying that they made them more social by making them more truly and profoundly human:

> When the small number of priests or the needs of the day demanded it, legions of apostles, eminent for their piety and learning, were seen issuing forth from the cloisters, who, by their valiant cooperation with the bishops, exerted the happiest influence on society, by putting an end to feuds, stifling enmity, bringing people back to the thought of duty, and by setting up again in honor the principles of religion and Christian civilization. (AMC, 497)

Theirs were deeds not of ideology but of love, the only thing capable of really uniting rich and poor, young and old, man and woman, ruler and subject, neighbor and neighbor.

In France, the religious congregations vied with one another in education, in works of charity, in spiritual acts of mercy. They were a glory to their country, and their disappearance, Pope Leo says, would "bring on the country an irreparable loss," not only in terms of what we call public assistance. For "an eloquent preaching of brotherhood and concord would be silenced" (AMC, 498). Brotherhood—*fraternité*, one of the three watchwords of the French revolutionaries! It is easy to practice the brotherhood of mankind. What is hard is to be a brother to the unhappy or unpleasant or ungrateful person next door. But this is just what the French congregations do, "without allowing the unpleasantness of their work or the ingratitude they may meet with to dampen their courage or check their ardor."

Yet they were not content to remain only within their own country. Here the congregations teach us a sobering lesson. Modern man is, said Richard Weaver, essentially a plutocrat. Whether he has money or not, he bows down before that idol, believing that Mammon alone has the power to cure all ills. If there are hungry people in the Sudan, he sends Mammon to the Sudanese government, and that alone must heal them; that must be their cure. Sad cure. For the more aching need is not the belly's, but the soul's. People who live under a government content to watch them starve need energetic and saintly people among them who are not content to watch them starve. They need more than money for food. They need *people*, to feed them in friendship.

That is what the French provided, says the Pope. "Exiles of their own free will," he says—and we should remember that this was a time when people still loved their native land most dearly—"the French missionaries go out across stormy sea and sandy desert seeking to gain souls for Christ in the most distant and often unexplored regions" (AMC, 499). Notice that the first thing comes first. We love our neighbor, or rather we make the savage in the wilds our neighbor and love him, not out of some reductive humanitarian requirement, but because he, that one there and no other, is who he is, a child of God, inexpressibly worthy of love. Teaching, feeding, and tending the sick are but expressions of that primal love, which says, as Josef Pieper puts it, "How good it is that you exist!" And so the missionaries "are seen settling amongst savage tribes in order to civilize them by teaching the elements of Christianity, the love of God and their neighbors, work, regard for the weak, and cleanly living." Unlike the humanitarian, whose money or whose worship of international political projects keeps him at a safe distance from those who suffer his patronage, these missionaries dwell with the people, and do so "without looking for any earthly reward even till death, which is often hastened by fatigue, the difficulties of the Church, or the sword of the executioner."

To the charge that "private charity" cannot possibly fulfill the role of the State in ameliorating the lives of those who suffer, we must answer again that that puts things exactly backward. In the first instance, the State has no wealth of its own to administer but must confiscate its funds from the work of private citizens themselves. Second, the State, by consuming the functions of truly social bodies that do work nearest to the people who participate in them, renders the people less and less able to unite to care for one another, and thus it helps to produce the pathologies it pretends to cure. But the most important point here is that we are not talking about private charity! We are talking about vigorous *public* action by a vigorous *public* body. Following the commands of their divine Founder, "those who embraced Christianity originated that wonderful variety of institutions for alleviating all the miseries by which mankind is afflicted" (GDC, 487).

Did they meet with the gratitude of the secular leaders? Let Leo sum up the situation as he writes on the silver jubilee of his pontificate:

> It is a great grief for Us to recall here the odious measures which were so undeserved and so strongly condemned by all honest men by which the members of religious orders were lately overwhelmed. Nothing was of avail to save them, neither the integrity of their life which their enemies were unable to assail, nor the right which authorizes all natural associations entered into for an honorable purpose, nor the right of the constitutions which loudly proclaimed their freedom to enter into those organizations, nor the

favor of the people who were so grateful for the precious services rendered in the arts, in the sciences, and in agriculture, and for the charity which poured itself out upon the most numerous and poorest classes of society. (*PAA*, 574)

Liberty was but a word on a piece of paper. Help for the poor was but a slogan on the lips of a politician. For "men and women who had spontaneously renounced all the joys of family to consecrate to the good of their fellow men, in those peaceful associations, their youth, their talent, their strength, and their lives, were *treated as malefactors as if they had formed criminal associations*, and have been excluded from the common and prescriptive rights at the very time when men are speaking loudest of liberty." So Pope Leo writes to the French president in 1883, deploring the expulsion of the religious orders from the institutions they had founded: "French citizens, whom the Church herself had in a way nourished and raised up with a motherly care in every kind of virtue and culture, to whom the nation owed her remarkable progress in knowledge sacred and profane and in the moral and religious education of her people, have been driven out of their peaceful refuges and been forced to seek a refuge far from their native land" (*Les Evenements*, 2588; my translation).

In our own time, religious organizations and orders fighting for natural marriage are said to be so filled with hatred that merely to associate with them makes one unfit for civilized society—makes it just for one to be driven out of work.

But where is that great variety of religious associations and orders now? We await their return. The social teaching of the Church requires a Church of societies, and in many places in a world of wealth and alienation, she will be the only creator of societies left.

6

The Church as Society

For to one is given by the Spirit the word of wisdom; to
another the word of knowledge by the same Spirit; to another
faith by the same Spirit; to another the gifts of healing by the
same Spirit; to another the working of miracles; to another
prophecy; to another discerning of spirits; to another divers
kinds of tongues; to another the interpretation of tongues;
but all these worketh that one and the selfsame Spirit, divid-
ing to every man severally as he will. For as the body is
one, and hath many members, and all the members of that
one body, being many, are one body: so also is Christ.
—1 Corinthians 12:8-12

And I saw no temple therein: for the Lord God
Almighty and the Lamb are the temple thereof.
And the city had no need of the sun, neither of
the moon, to shine in it: for the glory of God did
lighten it, and the Lamb is the light thereof.
—Revelation 21:22-23

I lead a double life. I am a Roman Catholic in the modern university.

It need not have been a double life. The Church, after all, invented the university, and before professors became mere researchers or educational functionaries, they were *professors*; that is, they professed something. They formed a special guild. Some of them, it's true, would be fishing in the river with a stick and a string and sleeping under a bridge were it not for the university, that haven for the unworldly. But many of them gave up the chance for success in the world, to pursue a holy aim—truth. They still don, a couple of times a year, the regalia that reminds us that, long ago, these people were a kind of priesthood.

I speak of traces here, hardly visible. And one evening my two lives met in a way that was both joyful and disconcerting. One of my dearest students, who had arrived at our college not believing in anything—and whose father who abandoned him and his mother when he was a boy—entered the Church. He and three others, that second Sunday after Easter, were baptized. Twelve more received Confirmation. About two hundred students showed up for the Mass, to rejoice with them. The choir sang their hearts out. Even a few professors were among all those *professors*! The wise and patient Dominican priest who had shepherded him through some dark valleys in the last two years was one of the concelebrants. He gave the young man his first Communion.

And there we all were, in the pleasant warmth of a spring evening, standing outside the chapel, greeting one another, jesting, embracing, laughing, congratulating the newborn lad, when all at once the priest flung out his arms and cried, "I love this place!"

And I was strangely aware that we were only a short walk from these classrooms, those offices, this sidewalk where professors and students proceed to their appointed rounds, this building where the Faculty Senate meets all the time, and I knew somehow this most beautiful and significant event did not touch the people who did not belong to the society that is the Church. I wanted to cry, "Come in, come in, join us, be at your ease! Here is the food and drink you've been longing for! The more, the merrier!"

When I visit a college where the Catholic Faith is heartily alive, I've come to see that I'm not visiting a *place*, or an institution, or an organization. What I find is more human than that, and far more exciting. I am visiting a *college*, a society of comrades *bound together* in allegiance to Christ and the truth. Others are colleges in name only.

I recall the first time it happened, at Christendom College, in northern Virginia. I had thought I'd visit to learn what a Catholic college would be like, and instead I learned first of all what a real *college* is like. The chapel was full for Mass at 11:30 in the morning, and no classes or office appointments were scheduled for that time. The cafeteria was full for lunch at 12:30, and again, no classes or office appointments were scheduled for that time. Everyone could go to Mass, and a lot of everyone did — professors, secretaries, the president of the college and his wife and children, other people's spouses and their children, students, visitors, people from town, everyone. Then at lunch everyone went to the same big room, chose from the same meals of the day, and sat at the same long tables, professors and students and other people mingling by happy chance; and a student mounted the stage to read announcements to the whole college. One of those was the opportunity to bid for dinner at the president's house — to raise money for the school, *their school*, where they did all these ordinary human things together, in the light of Christ.

Order among the Members of the Body

I've been maintaining that it is impossible to discuss Catholic social teaching without specifying what Catholics understand as a *society*. I've also insisted upon the wise dictum of St. Thomas, that grace perfects nature, which alone suffices to instruct the attentive Catholic that to sever faith from civic life is artificial and unnatural. We've looked at one of the two societies that the Pope holds up for our affection and admiration: the Christian family. Now it is time to look at the form of the Church.

Far from seeing religion as a pleasant decoration superadded to civil society, the Pope affirms that "religion, and religion only, can create the social bond" (AMS, 1892). History — and remember, Leo is a historian with a long and broad vista — teaches us as much. The key word in his sentence is *bond*. This *bond* is more profound than the phantom "contracts" dreamed by Hobbes, Locke, and their followers. A contract is a binding guarantee that we enter into because we *cannot trust* our fellow man to do the right thing. It is based upon suspicion. Without the contractual State, Hobbes says, mankind lapses into a war of "all against all," and the life of man is "solitary, poor, nasty, brutish, and short."

But Leo sees another dimension, the moral and spiritual depth of man — what makes it impossible for us to reduce him to his material wealth and appetites. I enter a contract, for self-serving and limited purposes; but I forge a bond. The bond is personal, engaging the whole of my being. And the social bond aims at the good of that whole human being, as we've seen: at his *moral improvement.*

Let's pause there. Time and again, Pope Leo, his keen mind making use of nineteen centuries of Christian history and thought, not to mention the sacred word of God, takes up the surgeon's probe and finds the diseased tissue. We hear people say that law cannot impose morality. That's nonsense, because that is what laws mainly do. But Leo says more. It is precisely for our *moral improvement* above all that we form societies in the first place. "Otherwise," he says—and did he enter a time machine to inspect the United States in 2012?—"society would rise but little above the level of an aggregation of beings devoid of reason, and whose whole life would consist in the satisfaction of sensual instincts." If that's what "society" has become, a highly organized anti-society, why join it at all? "Without this moral improvement it would be difficult to demonstrate," says Leo, "that civil society was an advantage rather than a detriment to man, as man." We would be savages in suits, but without the compensation of a sky above and the joy of the hunt.

Yet he says even more. The Church *is herself the consummate society.* That is why she does not cast her lot with any particular form of government, but regards them all as valid so long as they promote the common good: "The right to rule is not necessarily, however, bound up with any special mode of government. It may take this or that form, provided only that it be of a nature to insure the general welfare" (*ID*, 109; Leo's words are *boni communis*, the common good; more than general welfare, it is a good that is good by being shared). Therefore the Church *does not subject herself to the political form of the day.* She does not hang on the lips of political theorists. Nations rise and fall, but "only the Church of Jesus Christ has been able to preserve, and surely will preserve unto the consummation of time, her form of government." She has received from Christ, "who was, who is, and who will be forever," everything she needs for carrying out her mission in the midst of historical chances and changes.

If we ask what makes the Church this perfect society, marred by sin but glorious, black but beautiful, the answer, I believe, must be found in Christ's twin commandment. We are to love the Lord our God with all our heart and soul and mind and strength, and to love our neighbor as ourselves. The second commandment, says Jesus, is like unto the first; it is the application of the first to our action in the world. He who does not love his brother does not love God, says St. John, for God is love (1 John 4:8). The converse is also true. He who does not love God cannot love his neighbor *as himself*. He may feel affection for those of his neighbors who please his temperament, but that is no real bond. The grace-enabled heroism demanded by Christian charity will not be his.

But love, note well, does not insist upon equality. It is not narrow-eyed, searching out every shade of advantage or superiority and seeking to eliminate them, or to deny their value. Envy and resentment speak the language of equality, but love rejoices in the exuberant and, so to speak, immoderate blessings of God. Love always desires more and more for the beloved.

The Church admits everyone to her bosom, for in Christ, as St. Paul says, "there is neither Jew nor Greek, there is neither bond nor free, there is neither male nor female" (Gal. 3:28). A woman who is baptized is just as much a member of the Body of Christ as is a man; a slave, just as much as a master; a Greek, just as much as a Jew. Yet the same St. Paul says that God has "set the members every one of them in the body, as it hath pleased him" (1 Cor. 12:18). That means that not every member will be called for the same blessings: "Are all apostles? are all prophets? are all teachers? are all workers of miracles?" (1 Cor. 12:29).

A body is not a collective. It is not an undifferentiated mass. It is not a machine, whose parts work in concert because they are contiguous but otherwise have nothing to do with one another. The body is present in full in every member, and every member is for itself by being for the whole body. The health of the hand is good for the body, and the health of the body is good for the hand. Gifts granted to one member of the body redound to the others, because each member is for the others, so that "there should be no schism in the body; but that the members should have the same care one for another" (1 Cor. 12:25).

One of those gifts is hierarchical authority.

So Pope Leo writes to the archbishop of Paris (June 17, 1885) on the obedience that Catholic writers owe to the Church and her teachings. Among the other things that weigh heavily upon his heart, he says, one of the heaviest is that, "perhaps because of the vices of the times, there are those who are not content with the role of subjects that is theirs in the Church, but believe they can play a part in governing her also, or if not that, suppose that they may examine and judge by their lights the acts of her authority" (translations mine). But this is *un rovesciare l'ordine, e' portare in molti spiriti la confusione, e' uscire fuori di strada: to overturn order, to usher confusion in among many souls, to stray from the path.* Elsewhere he cites with approval the maxim of St. Cyprian: "Where the people are one with the priest, and the flock cleave to their Shepherd, there is the Church" (CMS, 2114; translation mine).

The self-styled progressive may respond by asserting that his deepest allegiance is not to some stated decree regarding virtue

or truth *now*, but to the *direction* that the decree can be seen
to take. As long as democratic machinery seems to run in that
direction, then "democracy" is valued above tradition, even
above truth: for there are no settled truths. It is fascinating to
note how exclusivist and antidemocratic such a position is. For
instance, those who studied and deeply appreciated Vatican II's
warnings and bold reaffirmations of Catholic doctrine are not
among the elites who are working "in the Spirit of Vatican II."
Their votes do not count. What Chesterton called "the democracy of the dead"—not traditionalism but a humble willingness
to continue to hear what our forebears have to say to us—is
eliminated. Their votes do not count either. A Pius XI, for
instance, is honored according to the degree to which he seems
to have anticipated the changes we favor, while the rest of his
pronouncements can be ignored.

Pope Leo will not allow it, or its strange counterpart, a refusal
to submit to a current Pope because of a supposed adherence to
a past Pope: "It is a hardly sincere argument of submission to
establish as it were an opposition between pontiff and pontiff."
There are some (the Old Catholics who broke with Pope Pius
IX over his pronouncement of the dogma of papal infallibility)
who will not deign to obey the current authority because they
hold to the past, and "in some ways they resemble those who
are condemned but who would appeal to a future Council or a
Pope who will be better informed." But Jesus Christ established
a Church, not a cabal of fortune-tellers.

Ultimately, for the Pope, it is a question of the one virtue that
can bind together the members of the Body of Christ: "What
results from forgetting these principles [of Church governance]
is the dwindling, among Catholics, of the respect, the reverence, and the trust in him who has been given to them as their

guide; and the loosening of that bond of love and submission, which should bind all the faithful to their shepherds, and the faithful and shepherds both to the supreme Shepherd; in which bond subsists most of all their common security and salvation." To deny this unity is, Leo says, most pernicious in these times, because the enemies of the Church have leagued together against her. It does not appear to me that our times are any less hostile to the Church; so that the Pope's call for unity in the ranks of Catholics is as timely as ever.

We should not be ashamed to acknowledge authority, which flows both from the Church to the world and, within the Church, from its Head, Jesus Christ, to its members. Authority, in its own right, is both necessary and blessed. Hence, men who provoke *novas rerum conversiones*, "fresh disturbances," new overturning of things, revolutions, are, in Leo's view, "full of treachery," and the source of the evils lies in this: "that the holy and venerable authority of the Church, which in God's name rules mankind, upholding and defending all lawful authority, has been despised and set aside" (*I*, 10). The Church must be given liberty to act, because "the cause of the public good and the well-being of all human society in general are also at stake" (*I*, 15). But the Church in no way seeks to reserve all power to herself. Because she upholds authority itself, she sees legitimate authority as a holy thing wherever it may be found. Because she is herself a society, and the model for societies, she helps to preserve society by protecting its order.

That explains why Leo looks with suspicion upon the principle of non-rule, which asserts that law depends upon the willingness of people to obey it: "As men are by the will of God born for civil union and society, and as the power of rule is so necessary a bond of society that, if it be taken away, society must at once be broken up, it follows that from Him who is the Author of society has come also the authority to rule; so that whosoever rules, he is the minister of God. Wherefore, as the end and nature of human society so requires, it is right to obey the just commands of lawful authority, as it is right to obey God who ruleth all things" (HG, 98). If we are talking about a genuine society and not a bureaucratically controlled aggregate, it "must have a ruling authority, and this authority, no less than society itself, has its source in nature, and has, consequently, God for its author" (ID, 109).

This need for authority springs also from the obvious differences among men. Leo says: "As the abilities of all are not equal, as one differs from another in the powers of mind or body, and as there are very many dissimilarities of manner, disposition, and character, it is most repugnant to reason to endeavor to confine all within the same measure, and to extend complete equality to the institutions of public life" (HG, 98). Now, to say that "all public power must proceed from God" (ID, 109) is not to deify that power, but to see its authority as rooted in, and dependent upon, its subordination to God, and to the ends for which God has made man.

I have often heard the nostrum, "Question authority," but never heard the much wiser nostrum, "Distinguish the true authority from the false." For authorities there must be. When the Russian emperor Alexander II, a courageous social reformer, was murdered by nihilists, Pope Leo responded with the encyclical *Diuturnum* (1881), whose first word suggests, so early in his reign, a frank appraisal of the hostility against the Church, now extending to hostility against authority *per se*. "The long-continued war waged against the divine authority of the Church," he begins his letter, "has reached the culmination to which it was tending, the common danger, namely, of human society, and especially of the civil power on which the public safety chiefly reposes" (141). That extension was inevitable, "for an unwillingness to attribute the right of ruling to God, as its Author, is no less than a willingness to blot out the greatest splendor of political power and to destroy its force" (151). Yet that is but to trade one lord for another; the true Lord of heaven and earth for the enslaving Enemy below; the legitimate earthly authority, for the misrule of lusts: "Although man, when excited by a certain arrogance and contumacy, has often striven to cast aside the reins of authority, he has never been able to arrive at the state of obeying no one" (142-143).

Religion does not need democracy, but democracy most certainly needs religion, to clear from people's heads the notion that they are, individually or collectively, their own sovereigns; to remind them that men discover the truth, and do not invent it; to provide them a just claim against tyranny, whether the tyrant is one or three hundred million in concert; to advise them that consent to a prudential measure is not the same thing as the creation of morality out of whole cloth; to teach them the piety and the patriotism that no number of bare contracts can enforce; and to give them a reason for loving their fellow countrymen, so as to make a true society, rather than a multitude of people essentially alienated from one another, who hate the law and hate their lawgivers but use the law as a weapon against their neighbors.

We Do Not Choose the Church

I have long heard that the Church needs to become more "democratic." This clamor for democracy comes in various forms, some mild and inoffensive, some legitimate, and some entirely mistaken. Some people want the faithful to be able to choose their bishops, as the people of Milan acclaimed St. Ambrose, and the people of Rome acclaimed Gregory the Great, against his will. The sense of the faithful, then, was that these men were holy and energetic soldiers of Christ. In other words, they were acclaiming men who would be their *leaders*, not their employees; men who would show them the true path to walk, not men who would favor the path the people wanted to walk. It was, we might say, a genuinely popular acknowledgment of the aristocrats of holiness in their midst.

But the idea that the people — lay or clergy — can subject the law of Christ to a plebiscite, under the pretext of "progress," pretending to possess some vague "spirit" of renewal, would simply burn the Church down to the roots. It would then *cease to be a society at all*. Leo is clear about this in his letter on Christian democracy, *Graves de communi*: "It is abhorrent to the profession of a Christian for any one to be unwilling to be subject and obedient to those who rule in the Church, and first of all to the bishops whom (without prejudice to the universal power of the Roman Pontiff) *the Holy Ghost has placed to rule the Church of God which Christ has purchased by His blood*" (GDC, 484; cf. Acts 20:28).

Can Catholics then unite among themselves to promote the kingdom of God? Of course they can and should, says Leo, yet always "with due regard to Episcopal authority and absolutely under Episcopal guidance" (*GDC*, 493). That authority is meant for their protection above all. For if you allow yourself to be carried away even by zeal for charitable works, and grow "wanting in proper submission," says Leo, "it is not a sincere zeal; it will not have any useful result and cannot be acceptable to God." We cannot steal ahead of the providence of God. We cannot pretend to know the leaders He will give us; we can only know the leaders He has given us, whom we must obey in all things *just*. That is to act as a member of the body, for the body. God "delights in the souls of those who put aside their own designs and obey the rulers of His Church as if they were obeying Him; He assists them even when they attempt difficult things and benignly leads them to their desired end."

The danger of the democratic spirit—I am not speaking here about the mechanics of voting—is that great men will be brought down to size, for the people, believing that authority springs from their consent alone, may not wish to acknowledge virtues that they themselves do not possess. How can the Church preach to people who breathe that air? Pope Leo had to deal with this question directly, raised by loyal churchmen in the vigorous young republic called the United States of America.

The question comes in three forms. The first and milder form is this, as Pope Leo states it in his 1899 letter to Cardinal Gibbons, *Testem benevolentiae*: "In order the more easily to bring over to Catholic doctrine those who dissent from it, the Church ought to adapt herself somewhat to our advanced civilization, and, relaxing her ancient rigor, show some indulgence to modern popular theories and methods" (*TB*, 442). That is, some accommodation to the democratic spirit is advisable for prudential reasons. We want people to listen to what we have to say, but they will not give us a hearing so long as we present to their view a forbidding palisade of moral laws and ecclesiastical precepts.

The Pope sensed the danger in this policy, which looks like charity but which springs instead from a denial of the Cross. "Those who dream of, and openly prefer, some discipline of thought and action in Christianity, with precepts less rigorous and more indulgent to human nature, that would demand of us to put up with little or nothing … have no notion of the spirit of faith and of Christian institutions, they do not see *the cross* meets us everywhere as the standard of life and the banner under which we must always fight if we would follow Christ, not in name only, but in deed and truth" (*T*, 473). Christ is no delegate, no leader we have chosen by our good grace. He is our King; and therefore "there is nothing servile in serving Christ our Lord with the understanding" (*T*, 472). Our society and its pastimes and passions do not dictate to the Lord; rather "Christ our Lord must be reinstated as the ruler of human society. All the elements of our commonwealth; legal commands and prohibitions, popular institutions, schools, marriage, home-life, the workshop, and the palace, all must be made to come to that fountain and imbibe the life that comes from Him" (*T*, 476).

So he advises Cardinal Gibbons to dilute nothing, to hold nothing in reserve. For just as Christ is the same yesterday, today, and tomorrow, so His laws, preached by the Church, are meant for men of every age and nation. They are salutary; and why withhold a healing remedy from those who need it most—namely, those who are least likely to know they need it? The Pope is quite prescient here: "Far be it, then, for any one to diminish or for any reason whatever to pass over anything of this divinely delivered doctrine; whosoever would do so, would rather wish to alienate Catholics from the Church than to bring over to the Church those who dissent from it" (*TB*, 443).

The Church "has never disregarded the manners and customs of the various nations which it embraces" (*TB*, 444), and that is simply another way of saying that all human cultures capture some portion of what is good and true, so that evangelism cleanses it from error and degradation, blesses it, and elevates it to a grandeur never known before. That is what the Church did for the ancient Romans, and it is what the Church can still do, and desires most ardently to do, for contemporary Americans. But she does so not by becoming more "American." She does so by making Americans most themselves, that is, Christian. In the matter of discipline, the Church shows herself to be a merciful mother, following the dictum of St. Paul: *I became all things to all men, that I might save all* (cf. 1 Cor. 9:22). In the matter of doctrine, and of the moral law, there can no more be compromise than there can be an alternate Christ.

The second form of the democrat's question is more troubling. It is asked whether democratic sensibilities should determine "the doctrines in which the *deposit of faith* is contained" (*TB*, 442). Some doctrines should be passed over in silence. This neglect is portrayed as a championing of the laity. So the Pope writes, gently and firmly, to the American cardinal:

> In the matter of which we are now speaking, Beloved Son, the project involves a greater danger and is more hostile to Catholic doctrine and discipline, inasmuch as the followers of these *novelties* judge that a certain liberty ought to be introduced into the Church, so that, limiting the exercise and vigilance of its powers, each one of the faithful may act more freely in pursuance of his own natural bend and capacity. (*TB*, 444)

The emphasis in that sentence is mine: Leo's Latin words are *rerum novarum*, new things, or, with their true linguistic coloration, *revolutionary things, things never known before.* Such things are naturally suspect, since God does not alter with the times. But Leo also says that the novelties spring from a false notion of liberty. Far from believing that liberty ought to be introduced *into* the Church, Leo reminds us that liberty comes *from* Christ and

His Church, because liberty is the unimpeded capacity to attain to that perfection for which we were made, union with God.

So for a people who cry, "Liberty, liberty," and mean permission to do as they like, the teaching authority of the Church, which truly is liberating, is needed all the more: "The license which is commonly confounded with liberty; the passion [Latin *libido*: lust] for saying and reviling everything; the habit of thinking and of expressing everything in print, have cast such deep shadows on men's minds, that there is now greater utility and necessity for this office of teaching than ever before, lest men should be drawn away from conscience and duty" (*TB*, 445). Leo welcomes gladly every real benefit that the genius of his age confers upon man, but none of it will be really useful, he says, without "the authority and wisdom of the Church."

An ontological collapse occurs in the Church when authority is despised. Again, Leo is not describing a historical result as much as a logical necessity: "They who take from Christian doctrine what they please lean on their own judgments, not on faith; and not *bringing into captivity every understanding unto the obedience of Christ*, they more truly obey themselves than God" (*Satis Cognitum*, 368; emphasis in the original translation; cf. 2 Cor. 10:5). Leo cites Augustine to conclude that such pickers and choosers — the underlying idea in the Greek word *haeresia* — do not actually believe the gospel, but believe themselves.

What's lost is the society itself. Again, this warrants some attention. If "society" is simply what we call a multitude of individuals, each picking and choosing what ecclesial practice or what statutory law will best fit his predilections, then there is no real society at all. If "justice" is only what Bob, Steve, and Sarah agree upon, in contract, each to further his own ends, with a protective proviso that no one will encroach upon the other, what is that, really, but a compact in mutual isolation?

But the most virulent form of the democratic question is to suggest that there is, so to speak, no aristocracy in the Church at all; no great saints whose lives we emulate; no heroic witnesses among us in the consecrated religious life. The Church democrat therefore rejects authority, "for the Holy Ghost, they say, pours greater and richer gifts into the hearts of the faithful now than in times past; and by a certain hidden instinct teaches and moves them *with no one as an intermediary*" (*TB*, 446; emphasis mine). The Latin reads *medio nemine*: no one, as it were, intruding between the individual and the Spirit.

The first problem with this assertion is its absurdity and its ingratitude. Leo, as always, is guided by the example of great men and women of faith who have gone before us: "For who when going over the history of the apostles, the faith of the rising Church, the struggles and slaughter of the valiant martyrs, and finally most of the ages past so abundantly rich in holy men, will presume to compare the past with the present times and to assert that they received a lesser outpouring of the Holy Ghost?" (*TB*, 446). But a deeper problem is that the assertion is itself antisocial! The saints do not tread upon the common man's corns. They summon him, they inspire him, they teach him, they lead the way. And mainly they lead the way by their cheerful and expansive and noble obedience. For "God in His infinite providence has decreed that men for the most part should be saved by men; hence He has appointed that those whom He calls to a loftier degree of holiness should be led thereto by men" (*TB*, 447).

Nor should we ever despise the holy life of consecrated nuns and brothers and priests, calling it merely passive, and suited for times past but not for now. "There is not," says Leo, "and cannot be a virtue which is really passive" (*TB*, 448), for virtue is a power, a dynamic habit oriented toward the primally good action, which is the submission of our free will to our liberator, God. But "from this species of contempt of the evangelical virtues, which are wrongly called *passive*, it naturally follows that the mind is imbued little by little with a feeling of disdain for the religious life," which supposedly must "narrow the limits of human liberty," and which is "better adapted to weak minds than to strong ones" (*TB*, 449). If the strong wish to try it, let them! For "those who, not content with the common duties of the precepts, enter of their own accord upon the evangelical counsels, in obedience to a divine vocation, present themselves to Christ as His prompt and valiant soldiers," and these soldiers "are so far from throwing away their liberty that they enjoy a nobler and fuller one—that, namely, *by which Christ has set us free*" (*TB*, 450; cf. Gal. 4:31).

Hence does Leo evaluate making democracy the standard by which we judge the Church, rather than the Church the standard by which we judge democracy. If we set democracy up as our idol, we must inevitably find ourselves outside of the very society we said we wished to promote. If religion is the only thing that can transform democracy into a real society, democracy can yet turn the Church into a bickering multitude of self-alienated people. To appeal to Catholic social teaching as an excuse for violating half of the catechism is like appealing to freedom of expression for blowing up the public library. It is antisocial.

That is especially true in our time, when the Western democracies, fiscally and culturally, have gone quite insane. "It raises the suspicion," says Leo of this attachment to democracy, "that there are some among you who conceive of and desire a church in America different from that which is in the rest of the world" (*TB*, 452). It cannot be. It is a contradiction in terms. Christ has no doppelgänger. He is One, and His Church is one.

7

Work

*And Isaac digged again the wells of water, which
they had digged in the days of Abraham his father;
for the Philistines had stopped them after the death
of Abraham: and he called their names after the
names by which his father had called them.*
—Genesis 26:18

*When I consider thy heavens, the work of
thy fingers, the moon and the stars, which thou
hast ordained; what is man, that thou art mind-
ful of him? And the son of man, that thou hast visited
him? For thou hast made him a little lower than the
angels, and hast crowned him with glory and honor.
Thou madest him to have dominion over the works of
thy hands: thou hast put all things under his feet.*
—Psalm 8:3-6

W hy do we work, other than that we must, to earn our daily bread?

There's a remarkable painting by the seventeenth-century Spanish artist Bartolomé Esteban Murillo that may teach us a great deal. It is of the Holy Family, within their small house. Mary is to our left, looking sideways with a calm and thoughtful glance and just the trace of a smile. She is unspooling thread. A basket of cloth lies by her feet. A small loom stands in the background, with threads draped upon it. Perhaps she is doing the mending. Joseph has paused from his labor. We can see, in the background on the right, a work table, a chisel, and a cross-cut saw. He is sitting on his bench, but he's not facing the table. He is facing us and, at an angle, Mary. He's holding in his arms the toddler Jesus — they are playing a little game. Jesus holds up in one hand a small bird, and a little white dog, evidently very intelligent, sits before them, looking toward Jesus' raised hand and "begging" with his right paw.

"Let us take our stand in front of that earthly and divine home of holiness, the house of Nazareth," writes Pope Leo (*Laetitiae sanctae* [1892], 209). "How much we have to learn from the daily life which was led within its walls! What an all-perfect model of domestic society! Here we behold simplicity and purity of conduct, perfect agreement and unbroken harmony, mutual respect and love — not of the false and

135

fleeting kind — but that which finds both its life and its charm in devotedness of service."

What is work for? It is for the same thing that everything else in our lives is for. It is for family and neighbors; it is for rest and celebration; it is for play; it is for prayer; it is for God.

Troubles of the Times

It is generally held that Catholic social teaching begins with Pope Leo XIII's masterly encyclical *Rerum novarum* (1891). That, as I've tried to show, is a dreadful mistake. Pope Leo considered it his duty to apply to current concerns the constant teaching of the Church and of the word of God. Like Thomas Aquinas, the study of whose works he so vigorously promoted, Leo would have considered "originality" a vice, not a virtue. But it is true in divine matters as in the arts. They who concentrate only on representing humbly and accurately what they see of the truth will end up being "original" without intending it, while they who seek originality end up peddling the same old reductive heresies that have plagued the Church from the beginning. "Seek ye the kingdom of God first," says Jesus, "and all these other things will be given to you also" (cf. Matt. 6:33).

Perhaps we are misled by the title *Rerum novarum*. In our anti-society of rapacious consumption of the "new" and "improved," and the unease instilled in us by mass marketers and politicians who cry that if we do not act now, we will be lost — "Awake, arise, or be forever fall'n!" cries the Prince of Politicians to his fellow devils in Milton's hell — we are apt to credit Pope Leo with seeing the light of novelty. No such thing. As I've observed, the ancient Romans held the political *innovator* to be a plague. *Res nova* means *revolution*, and the "spirit of revolutionary change," *rerum novarum spiritus*, writes Leo, has been disturbing the nations of the world. That spirit is more often roused by hatred of the all-too-visible past, especially its glories, than by any love for an always vague and invisible future.

What were the elements of this upheaval? Leo names five: "The vast expansion of industrial pursuits and the marvelous discoveries of science; the changed relations between masters and workmen; the enormous fortunes of some few individuals, and the utter poverty of the masses; the increased self-reliance and closer mutual combination of the working classes; the prevailing moral degeneracy" (*RN*, 208). The first is a neutral datum; it is the stage. The next three are social conditions with deep moral implications. The fifth is a moral sickness that would, unchecked, vitiate any attempt to solve the problems of the working classes by monetary or juridical means—we might say, by mechanical means.

How did matters come to this pass? Leo blames the secularism spreading like a contagion from one European nation to the next. He had made that charge in his earlier encyclicals. One after another, the institutions that once brought master and workman together have been weakened or destroyed. The guilds were abolished; Leo will, in his practical recommendations, return again and again to the model of the guild. For the guilds, founded in the Middle Ages, were social, economic, and religious all at once. Guildsmen trained the young in their trades; they maintained a high standard of quality; they provided stability in costs and profit; they cared for their invalid members and their widows and orphans; and they united in the worship of God, especially to celebrate their patronal feasts. "My liege," says the bluff Simon Eyre to King Henry VII in Thomas Dekker's *The Shoemaker's Holiday* (1599), "I am six and fifty year old, yet I can cry humph! with a sound heart for the honor of Saint Hugh."

Henry the Eighth had been dead and in his grave for many years, and his daughter Elizabeth would live only a few years more, and yet there was the playwright Dekker, writing as if it were the most natural thing in the world that men who worked the same craft would make merry on the feast day of their saint and intercessor.

But, says Leo, "the ancient workingmen's guilds were abolished in the last century" *(RN, 209)*. The word he uses is *collegiis*, colleges, bands of men in league together; not simply a union, but a genuinely human society of men with a common interest, living and working with one another. That abolition was of a piece with laws that "set aside the ancient religion," leaving nothing between worker and master: "Hence by degrees it has come to pass that workingmen have been surrendered, all isolated and helpless, to the hard-heartedness of employers and the *greed* of unchecked competition" (emphasis mine; Latin *cupiditati*: lust).

Matters are made all the worse by "rapacious usury, which, although more than once condemned by the Church, is nevertheless, under a different guise, but with the like injustice, still practiced by covetous and grasping men." I'm not qualified to comment on the Church's monetary realism, and the difference she sees between usury and, say, the profit a passive member derives from a joint stock corporation, or the fair price one may charge for ready and obvious opportunities forgone when one lends money to another. Nor can I now comment on the buying and selling of bundles of funds made up of purchases and sales of other funds or loans or bonds whereby people alive now fleece people yet to come, except to say that in our time the Church's hesitancy to accept usury as a fact of life now looks as if it could *only* have been inspired by the Holy Spirit. What I want to note is that for Leo, since we are talking about human beings made by

God and for God, the misery we cause one another cannot be cordoned off into compartments, one religious and one secular. Rapacity is a moral issue. The denigration of the Church is a moral issue. We are talking about *sin*.

Now one cannot cure sin by sin. Our Lord tells us: one cannot cast out devils in the name of Beelzebub. But this, Leo sees, is what some revolutionaries pretend to do: "To remedy these wrongs the socialists, *working on the poor man's envy of the rich*, are striving to do away with private property, and contend that individual possessions should become the common property of all, to be administered by the State or by municipal bodies" (emphasis mine). Leo does not condemn socialism for its practical failure, although he notes—was he granted a premonitory vision of Russia and Cuba and what used to be *Great* Britain?—that "the workingman himself would be among the first to suffer" (*RN*, 210). We must see the relationship aright. Socialism is not evil because it fails; it fails because it is evil. If that word sounds too harsh, let us just say that it is an evil system that tricks some well-intended people, seducing them with promises and causing them to overlook false principles. Nor can it be justified because unchecked rapacity is evil—the antisocial money-squeezing that Dickens, alike suspicious of socialists, condemned. One does not hire Belial to fight Beelzebub.

What Is to Be Done?

At this point, one might expect Leo to launch into economic analysis, and provide a "solution" to the trouble. But we must clear away the childishly bad thinking to which we have grown accustomed—our fetish for numbers. Man is a moral being to the core. Man is oriented by his nature toward God, with every breath he takes. We seek not money. We seek joy. A life of material comforts and moral indifference is unworthy of man; if the beasts could feel shame, they would be ashamed of that.

Instead the Pope returns to the nature of man. We work; we exercise our minds, as God commanded us even before the Fall. Man puts *himself* into his work, and so the reward of his work becomes his own, not the property of the State. Nor is this property held at the allowance of the State, reverting to the State at his decease. For, unlike the beasts, he dwells, as it were, above the current of time: "Man, fathoming by the faculty of reason matters without number, and linking the future with the present, becoming, furthermore, by taking enlightened forethought, master of his own acts, guides his ways under the eternal law and the power of God, whose providence governs all things" (*RN*, 211). His deeds, says Leo, do not die out. He makes his own "that portion of nature's field which he cultivates—that portion on which he leaves, as it were, the impress of his individuality" (*RN*, 213). That includes the land itself. If we consider the matter, all of human economy derives ultimately from something taken from the land or the sea and transformed into something useful or beautiful.

We must be careful here. Leo is making no assertion about the value that a man's work adds to an object. He is also not saying that it is work *alone* that makes a thing proper to the person who labors upon it. The right of private property is grounded, not in practical economics, but in the theomorphic nature of man. Neither a brute nor a robot can properly be said to *own* anything. Only persons can own, because only persons seal their creations with the stamp, not of their labor merely, but of their persons, the very selves that dwell in and beyond time. This is true regardless of whether we make what will last a thousand years, like a cathedral, or what will be consumed in a day, like a loaf of bread. Human labor must be honored not because it is labor, but because it is human.

Are we now ready to consider the State and laws established for the common good? By no means. It's a symptom of our secular disease that we idolize the untrammeled individual, motivated by one hedonism or another, whether of rapacity or lust, and the State established to adjudicate among the hedonists. Such a man is less than fully human, and such a State is at once greater than a true State, as a tumor outgrows the organ it supplants, and less than a State, in that it provides at best for a tolerably managed common-evil.

No, we must still remember what man is, man as a social being. He is made for love. In particular, he is made for that God-created society, the family. He is made for the scene painted by Murillo. Unchecked avarice may destroy families by depriving them of the material goods to which the workman rightly lays claim. But socialism destroys families by denying their very nature, and by usurping their functions: "The contention, then, that the civil government should at its option intrude into and exercise intimate control over the family and the household, is a great and pernicious error" (RN, 215).

Rapacity for wealth is not cured by rapacity for power. These things, then, are grave violations of Catholic social teaching, as formulated by Pope Leo XIII: to proceed as if the child were the ward of the State; to seize from parents the oversight of their children's education; to intrude the law into the family circle except when that circle has been broken by serious crime; to enact laws that encourage the dissolution of families; to enact laws that discourage the formation of families; to pretend that the basic definition of the family is the prerogative of individuals or the State; to treat monetary issues solely as between an individual and an individual, or an individual and the State, without regard to the family; to seize property from the family at the decease of its head; to relegate religion to the private sphere, so that the State, or the wealthy, or whatever aggregate may wield power, need not concern themselves with it.

Now then, how shall we ameliorate the lot of the working classes? I've written that one cannot enlist Belial to put down Beelzebub. One must not hire a slave driver to defeat a slave driver. The working classes must be *free*. But freedom, as we've seen, is far more than a negative against others. Freedom comes from God and finds its flourishing and its end in God. Law — the eternal law — is the precondition for human freedom. And just as grace perfects nature, just as the preaching of the gospel elevated the culture of the ancient pagans so that ordinary men and women attained to a heroic holiness that the very imaginations of such worthies as Pericles and Cicero could not reach, so too the law of the Church exalts the relation between labor and capital, between workingman and owner. We are not talking here about political leverage or about some abstract formula for the disposition of income. We are talking about human beings, and the righteous Judge they must one day face, to give a reckoning of their deeds, good and evil. "Exclude the idea of futurity," writes Leo, "and forthwith the very notion of what is good and right would perish" (RN, 220).

What We Owe to the Workman

Freedom apart from law is a delusion, and law originates in God. What, then, does religion teach the workman? He should deal honestly and fulfill all fair contracts. He should not damage the owner's property or threaten his person. No riots, no disorders, no communion with men of evil principles. And the owner? I'd like to cite this passage in full and mentally include all political leaders, teachers, advertisers, social workers; all who derive their livelihood from the work of the lower classes, or from their fealty, or their debility. I will also separate one directive from another:

1. Religion teaches the wealthy owner and the employer that their work-people are not to be accounted their bondsmen;

2. that in every man they must respect his dignity and worth as a man and as a Christian;

3. that labor is not a thing to be ashamed of, if we lend ear to right reason and to Christian philosophy, but is an honorable calling, enabling a man to sustain his life in a way upright and creditable;

4. and that it is shameful and inhuman to treat men like chattels to make money by, or to look upon them merely as so much muscle or physical power.

5. Again, therefore, the Church teaches that, as Religion and things spiritual and mental are among the workingman's main concerns, the employer is bound to see that the worker has time for his religious duties;

6. that he be not exposed to corrupting influences and dangerous occasions;

7. and that he be not led away to neglect his home and family, or to squander his earnings;

8. Furthermore, the employer must never tax his work-people beyond their strength, or employ them in work unsuited to their sex or age;

9. His great and principle duty is to give everyone a fair wage. (*RN*, 219)

Let us examine the directives here, one by one.

1. That workmen are not to be accounted as "bondsmen" seems easy enough. When my grandfather worked for the Hudson Coal Company, and an underground explosion nearly killed him—he lost one of his lungs—the owners of the company said that he was responsible for his own harm, since a couple of nearby coal-boys got out in time unscathed, and he didn't. They could get away with such injustice then. Nowadays they'd be settling a large lawsuit out of court.

But it is not clear to me that a company that treats its workers in such a brutal or shabby way is so much worse than a company that forgets that its workers are human beings at all. In other words, a company that hires *men* to work enters into a real human relationship, not only with the workers but with their families and with the cities and towns where they work. To ignore these is to fall down in worship of monetary profit. To justify it by appealing to the interest of the stockholders is to make them complicit in the crime. The presumption, because of what man is, must always be in favor of continuance and stability.

2. This directive is now almost incomprehensible to us, and more's the pity. Allow me to illustrate. In Richard Llewellyn's autobiographical novel of his childhood among the coal mines in Wales, *How Green Was My Valley*, the sons of the miner Gwilym Morgan tell their father that they should be expecting lower wages soon. The father, who detests the very idea of a union, asks why. They reply that ever since the iron works in the next valley closed down, many of the unemployed men have been coming

over looking for work in the mines. The demand for work, in other words, is greater than the supply; so the owners *can* offer less, and the iron workers will go for it rather than nothing.

"The owners will not do that," says Mr. Morgan.

"And why not, Father?"

"Because they are not savages. They are men, as we are."

"They are men, yes, but they are not as we, because they have power, and we do not."

Yet the boys are proven right, and the father wrong. The owners offer the lower wage, because they can get away with it. They have forgotten that they stand under the judgment of God. They have forgotten that the workmen are their brothers. In our day, it too rarely happens that the owner and his employees break bread together or bend the knee in prayer together. Nothing unites them but a bare contract, or what Thomas Carlyle called the *cash nexus*. That is not natural and not fully human.

3. We do not live to work, but there is a nobility to work nonetheless, and the Christian cannot forget that our Lord Himself worked with His hands at the plane and the lathe. The Man who lay in the remarkable Shroud of Turin was a broad-shouldered, imposing fellow.

In *Paradise Lost*, when the fallen Adam reconsiders the words of the Lord, that he should earn his bread by the sweat of his brow, he says, "Idleness had been worse." Nor was there idleness before the Fall, as Milton rightly shows. Adam and Eve tend the garden, using their choice and intelligence to make it more beautiful, more comfortable, more human a place.

If we could arrange it so that men would drink and eat and sleep, without work—if we could give them the income to allow for it—that must at best be a stopgap, a bridge from work to work. It need not be so, if human beings were only animals, but, as Gwilym Morgan says, we are not savages but men. We need to give of ourselves; even the poor need to give of themselves, and deserve to have their gifts received and honored.

4. It is always shameful to treat human beings as if they were mere machines. We make the same error if we treat them as mere feeders, creatures with animal needs alone. As always, the relationship must be *human*: which is not the same thing as *humanitarian*. It is not abstract and distant and ideological. It must be personal. Employer and employee stand in the sight of God; they are persons made in the image of God.

5. This directive also is nearly incomprehensible to us. But it was not so long ago that most businesses were closed on Sunday. As late as a few years ago, that was still the case in Nova Scotia, until the business interests finally won in a referendum. The only defense the opponents could make in secular Canada was that the day of general rest provided a time for families to get together with other families, and neighbors with neighbors.

We should not suppose that Pope Leo is indulging in something anachronistic here. The men of his day were made in the image and likeness of God. They owed worship and gratitude to God; not only as individuals but as a people. *That has not changed.* When an employer hires a worker, he hires someone who owes that worship to God. How that may be honored in the contract is a good question, given the kinds of work that sometimes must be done regardless of the day (police work, for example). *That* it must be honored is not in question.

6. The word that Pope Leo uses for *corrupting influences* is *lenociniis*: literally, whoring. The Church casts a cold eye on the

farming of jobs out to sweatshops in distant lands; and a cold eye on the sweaty stews in lands whose wealth is wasted on vice and folly. We must learn again to treat one another as the fully human beings we are, or should be.

The Church instructs us to avoid the near occasion of grave sin. We'd then have to avoid almost every workplace in our land. Convenience stores sell smut. Instructors in public schools teach it. Men and women in the army are thrust together in close quarters, with no regard to their moral welfare or the welfare of their families, let alone military advantage. Whole industries feed upon the weakness of the flesh; that includes the poverty industries. Far from encouraging continence before marriage and chastity and fidelity within it, the entertainment industry scoffs at such things and thus steals from the poor their main source of capital—which is not monetary but metaphysical and moral.

But one of the most pernicious ways in which those in power keep their workers or their clients where they are is to corrupt their morals. A worker who wastes his money on drink provided on the premises of the quarry or mine is a man who will be on a short leash, ever more beholden to the owners. We can see the dynamic at work nowadays by considering who provides most of the money for state-run lotteries and keno machines. They are not the rich but the relatively poor, especially working men hoping to strike it big. Thus, a company may be granted a consideration to place a keno machine on the premises. The company is essentially receiving a portion of the state's proceeds, while the state levies a surreptitious tax on those least able to afford it, all under the pretext of providing recreation. Meanwhile, the worker who drains his credit card down by playing the machine becomes ever more firmly bound to the state's ministrations and less likely to advance from his status as a laborer.

Pope Leo saw that the health of a State rests upon the moral strength of its people. But the State may be long in dying. And while it is dying, those who run the State—those whose money, cunning, or self-interested self-control give them some armor against the evils they encourage—may be content to keep the moral tenor of the people weak and effeminate, because they gain from the degradation directly and indirectly.

7. This directive is similar to the preceding, but it reminds us of something that, within living memory, had been taken as a matter of course: that is, the workman is never merely an individual. He represents a family—either a current or a prospective family. The Industrial Revolution brought about a severance between work and home. Most people until fairly recently worked in the same place where they lived. They lived on their farm, or they worked out of a shop that was part of the home. Pope Leo wishes to remind us that this severance is adventitious. Even if a man works far from where he lives, he works *for that family and for that home.* So he is not the only one who bears responsibility for them. The employer shares in that responsibility.

In those days, the typical way in which employers neglected that responsibility was, besides paying too little, requiring employees to work long hours, sixty or seventy a week. That was to squeeze from the orange as much juice as they could, given the labor market. It was based on a denial of human solidarity. You would never do such a thing to your brother. Why, then, would you do it to—your brother?

No one works those hours now without being paid handsomely. Yet more and more, employees are offered *strange hours* to work, at somewhat higher-than-average pay. One of the world's largest candy factories employed my mother-in-law and her fellows at a round-robin of strange hours, just to keep the machines running continually: two weeks on the day shift, two weeks on the swing shift, then two weeks on the night shift. They paid for it. So did the families—dearly.

8. This directive may seem quaint and utterly inapplicable to our times. As for children, Leo says, "great care should be taken not to place them in workshops and factories until their bodies and minds are sufficiently developed," lest "too early an experience of life's hard toil blight the young promise of a child's faculties" (*RN*, 234). It is not clear to me what Pope Leo would say about the mental anesthesia of our schools, where drudgery, moral degeneracy, and physical idleness go together.

We are, moreover, a society that now sends its women to face the bullets and hand grenades of enemies in war; one that arms women with guns to face murderers in our streets. Leo is too sensible a realist for such things. "A woman," he says, "is by nature fitted for home work, and it is that which is best adapted at once to preserve her modesty and to promote the good bringing up of children and the well-being of the family" (*RN*, 235).

As always, the *family*—that prime society—is first in Pope Leo's mind.

Relations between Rich and Poor

We come to the final and summary directive. The worker must be paid a *fair wage*.

To deny a fair wage—to deny a workingman a wage fit to support his family in a way becoming to a human being—is a "crime which cries to the avenging anger of Heaven." Now, to detach this sentence from the whole of Leo's moral and social vision is to commit the sin of the nineteenth-century liberals who justified low wages on utilitarian grounds. It is to forget *what man is*. It will not do, then, for a government to hand to some people money confiscated from other people, without taking any account of the ends for which we are made. What Leo is trying to do here is to *bind owner and workman together* in bonds that are personal and religious; something that mere human law cannot do. It will not serve to cure somebody of typhus if you are then going to infect him with pneumonia, scarlet fever, and tetanus.

Like Thomas Aquinas, whom he admired so well, Leo is quite practical. It is right for a man to provide for his family so that they may live in a "becoming" way, worthy of their high calling (*RN*, 222). That implies more than bare necessities. Think of the life of the Church. She is not Puritan. She does not follow the worldly and false asceticism of Judas, who complains that the adulteress has lavished too much on the ointment for Jesus' feet. The Church is not drab, nor does she enjoin dreariness upon her children. Our calendar is filled with feasts, and common people, over all these centuries, have delighted in adorning their places of worship with art and music and colorful celebrations.

Most people in America now have the means to live becomingly. But we spend inordinate—I use the word advisedly—resources on things that are neither necessary nor becoming; on things that hinder us on our pilgrimage to the celestial homeland and that make our villages and towns and cities, or what's left of them, less like comfortable way stations than like moral tar pits or bogs of quicksand. I'm not speaking here only of *material* superfluity. Teachers, professors, doctors, lawyers, advertisers, actors, athletes, journalists, social workers, and politicians possess a superfluity of *influence* far beyond what a landed gentleman in Leo's day possessed. And just as an unscrupulous merchant can corner a market to rifle the capital of the poor man, so too now the foolish and selfish who are rich in influence can, and do, rifle the metaphysical and moral capital of the poor—and gain materially and politically from the rifling. That theft is by far the wickeder, because eternal life is at stake.

The Church, says Leo, warns us that "abundance of earthly riches are no warrant for the bliss that shall never end, but rather are obstacles; that the rich should tremble at the threatenings of Jesus Christ—threatenings so unwonted in the mouth of Our Lord—and that a most strict account must be given to the Supreme Judge for all we possess" (*RN*, 221). It is a warning that is seldom heard now. We no longer know how to live modestly, or in decent and honorable poverty. My wife's grandparents lived for a while in a house with a packed dirt floor. But that house was in order nonetheless. "Not everybody can be rich," said her grandmother, "but everybody can be clean." Nor do we any longer sense the moral danger of wealth. It is telling that the Latin word that once described lust, *luxuria*, has undergone quite a transformation in modern English. At first it described a dishonorable attachment to lusts of the flesh: *lechery*. Now it describes what everyone craves without embarrassment: *luxury*. "How difficult it is," says Jesus, "for a rich man to enter the kingdom of heaven!" (cf. Matt. 19:23).

The Church does not deny a man's right to possess what is his. And Scripture gives us warrant for believing that wealth can be a blessing sent by God. But God sends His blessings to be *fruitful*. It is true, the merchant's money belongs to him; so too, I'll add, do non-monetary riches belong to those who are blessed with them. And not only is it evil to steal the rich man's goods; it is evil even to *desire them*. But "it is one thing to have a right to the possession of money, and another to have a right to use money as one wills." The word Leo employs here, for "right to use," is the legal term *usu*: to possess the money *does not imply a full moral title of use.*

If we set aside our eternal destiny and our Lord's commandments of charity, Pope Leo will seem to be contradicting himself. For he quotes Thomas again: "Man should not consider his outward possessions as his own, but as common to all, so as to share them without hesitation when others are in need" (*RN*, 222). This sharing is not a duty required by justice, says Leo, except "in extreme cases." Secular man knows no other duty, if even that one. But this is the duty of love—which human law cannot reach. To sum up: "*Whoever has received from the divine bounty a large share of temporal blessings, whether they be external and corporeal, or gifts of the mind, has received them for the purpose of using them for the perfecting of his own nature, and, at the same time, that he may employ them, as the steward of God's providence, for the benefit of others.*"

What is that benefit? We must not lose sight of this. A becoming life here, directed toward eternal life with God. Let me quote Pope Leo at length, in his encyclical recommending *the Holy Rosary* as a remedy for the ills of his time:

But men of carnal mind, who love nothing but themselves, allow their thoughts to grovel upon things of earth until they are unable to lift them up to that which is higher. For, far from using the goods of time as a help towards securing those which are eternal, they lose sight altogether of the world which is to come, and sink to the lowest depths of degradation. We may doubt if God could inflict upon man a more terrible punishment than to allow him to waste his whole life in the pursuit of earthly pleasures, and in forgetfulness of the happiness which alone lasts forever. (*LS*, 213)

People should not want for food and drink. That dire want is unbecoming a creature made in the image of the bountiful Father. But food and drink are not enough. When we observe the life of Jesus, says the Pope, we see that He has blessed forever the life of manual labor; we needn't be ashamed of it. And "from contemplation of this divine exemplar, it is more easy to understand that the true worth and nobility of man lies in his moral qualities, that is, in virtue" (*RN*, 223). This treasure is "the common inheritance of men, equally within the reach of high and low, rich and poor." Leo has chosen his words with great deliberation. One person may inherit a great estate; another may attend one of our prestigious colleges; but virtue is the true *common inheritance* of everyone. Consider what a sin it would be to snatch that inheritance away! But if instead we heeded the example and the teaching of Jesus, it would not be difficult "to make rich and poor join hands in friendly concord" and common sharing of that inheritance.

The concord is no mere abstraction. Leo has in mind a society wherein the rich man and the poor man are friends; they live near one another; they celebrate at the same festivals; they kneel beside one another in church; they know one another's children; they are *for one another*. Obviously, that cannot be produced by the mechanics of legislation, no more than love can be compelled. It is not enough that one pay high taxes, some smallish portion of which will filter to some unknown "poor" far away from one's sight and smell. It is worse still when concomitant laws make it exceedingly unlikely that those poor people will have any clear way to recover that common inheritance of moral

virtue that should be theirs—laws that, as I've suggested, discourage the formation and preservation of families, and facilitate
their dissolution, and rule out the Church, the only institution
on earth that can assist the poor against those long odds.

For the Church, Leo notes, assists the temporal welfare of
the poor directly, through alms, and indirectly, although more
effectively, by promoting Christian morality. We do not follow
God's commandments so as to gain comfort in this life. But those
commandments restrain "the greed of possession" and "the thirst
for pleasure"—twin engines of a diseased soul and a dying society
(*RN*, 226). They destroy us even amid abundance. Christian
morality, by contrast, can supply much of our want by means
of—note the word Leo uses—"economy," that is, the right governance of a household. It teaches us to be content with "frugal
living"—again, note the word. The *frugal* person makes full use
of the *fruits* nearby; thus is frugality a part of temperance and of
gratitude to God, lest we tread His gifts underfoot.

Now, if people are meant *for one another*, and if they generally
prosper by the natural virtues, then they should be free to form
associations to promote their temporal and moral welfare. The
Church has formed such associations from the beginning; she
has invented the hospital, the orphanage, the home for pension-
ers, schools for the indigent, and so forth—"deposits of piety,"
says Leo, quoting Tertullian; and again the financial metaphor
is apt. She begs on behalf of the beggars! She "has established
congregations of religious and many other useful institutions for
help and mercy, so that hardly any kind of suffering could exist
which was not afforded relief" (*RN*, 227). But the secularists of
Leo's day were working to force the Church out of her right role,
seeking to supplant charity with secular mechanisms. Nothing
has changed. We have seen, in the United States and Canada,

an aggressive attempt to squeeze the Church out of her schools, hospitals, colleges, adoption agencies, and other social services, unless she agrees to become what she is not, an appendage to the State, truckling to her false master, ashamed of the True. One cannot serve both God and Mammon.

Catholic social teaching demands full freedom for the Church and for free associations of Christians to do the only real work that can unite rich and poor—and to do so without interference by the State, and without reducing "welfare" to the mathematical and mechanical definition that is the only one the secular State can give. What is happening to Catholic schools in Ontario, what happened to the Catholic adoption agency in Massachusetts, what is going to happen to Catholic employers throughout the United States is a monumental betrayal of everything that Pope Leo XIII ever stood for.

There were people in Leo's time, as I've observed, who were at least honest in their contempt for the Church's charity. "They would substitute in its stead," says he, a system of relief organized by the State" (*RN*, 227). But, aside from the inhumanity of it all, that is to mistake the means for the end. The goods are the means. They cannot be the end, because we are talking about human beings and not brutes. "We have insisted that, since the end of society is to make men better"—the *perfectionnement morale* we have seen Leo promote as the reason we come together—"the chief good that society can possess is virtue" (*RN*, 229). That means that men must possess enough of the "bodily and external commodities *the use of which is necessary to virtuous action*" (*RN*, 229; emphasis in the original; cf. Thomas Aquinas, *De Regimine Principum*, 1.15).

What, then, should the State do? Let us turn now to that subordinate but important matter.

8

The State

Breathes there the man, with soul so dead,
Who never to himself hath said,
This is my own, my native land!
Whose heart hath ne'er within him burn'd,
As home his footsteps he hath turn'd,
From wandering on a foreign strand!
　　　—From Sir Walter Scott,
　　　　The Lay of the Last Minstrel

He doesn't make two blades of grass
the same: how much less two saints,
two nations, two angels.
　　　—From C. S. Lewis,
　　　　That Hideous Strength

One of the dearest of my boyhood memories was of Memorial Day, then commonly called Decoration Day, because it was the day when people went to decorate the graves of their departed kin. It was also the day when people honored the dead who had fought in America's wars.

We didn't do much in my town in those days, because real civic life had already been badly worn away by television, divorce, and the waning influence of the Church. But still, on Memorial Day, or Decoration Day, there would be a big parade, proceeding with trumpets and bugles and fifes, baton twirlers, fire trucks, and old veterans in uniform, first to the hill on one side of the town, where the Protestant cemetery lay, then to the hill on the other side of the town, where the Catholic cemetery lay. My cousins and I would get up early in the morning to be at the Protestant cemetery when the men got there. Everybody would fall silent; you would hear nothing but the wind or the robins in the trees. Then the sergeant at arms would bark out a command, and the old men would take their rifles from their sides, shoulder them, aim to the skies, and fire, three times. The smoke cleared away; the echoes fell silent. And someone would take up the bugle and play the solemn and mournful night call, Taps.

Then the parade would turn and proceed back down the hill, while the other boys and I clambered on top of one of the fire trucks, hitching a ride through town. The morning ended with

Reclaiming Catholic Social Teaching

Mass at the Catholic cemetery, followed by orange juice and doughnuts at the American Legion. Patriotism was good.

I mention these things because we are too quick to think of states and not nations; of laws as if they could be applied *ad libitum* to any group of people at any time, anywhere; as if some distilled justice could be visited upon any group, regardless of culture or material conditions; as if, for our discussion here, economics involved utility machines rather than human persons. The caveat is necessary. When we talk about "the State," we must never lapse into thinking that a solution that will work for one people in one culture must necessarily work for all. We must instead look at the *principles* that will characterize any solution, regardless of cultural circumstances. We must keep our eyes on the human beings — the boys riding the fire truck, the men firing their rifles, the grandmothers cheering the parade from their front porches, the women laying flowers upon the graves, and the beloved who lie beneath the grass. With that caveat, let us proceed.

Pope Leo XIII affirms that a well governed State will promote the material and moral prosperity of its citizens, will honor private property and free association, and will protect the poor from abuse or depredation by the rich.

How to do these things? Leo lays down four principles.

The first is what I'll call the Principle of Moral Health. "A State," he says, "chiefly prospers and thrives through moral rule, well-regulated family life [family life directed from within by the moral law], respect for religion and justice, the moderation and equal allocation of public taxes, the progress of the arts and of trade, [and] the abundant yield of the land — through everything, in fact, which makes the citizens better and happier" (*RN*, 228). The emphasis is on direction from the objective moral law, and on a combination of self-restraint and industriousness.

This self-restraint, when practiced by the State, suggests a second principle, what I'll call the Law of Sufficient Generality. A well-governed State will assist the poor primarily by establishing an environment wherein people of common decency and assiduousness can raise healthy children to become good citizens in their turn: "The more that is done for the benefit of the working classes by the general laws of the country, the less need will there be to seek for special means to relieve them."

That leads to the third, what I'll call the Principle of the Home. It's often called subsidiarity. We must never confuse a true beneficence, which honors the prime society of the family, with the false beneficence that barters goods in exchange for the family's soul: "The State must not absorb the individual or the family; both should be allowed free and untrammeled action so far as is consistent with the common good and the interests of others" (*RN*, 230). The same holds true of free associations. The State must "not thrust itself into their peculiar concerns and their organization" (*RN*, 243). There are practical reasons for this restraint. It is absurd to suppose, for example, that a flock of bureaucrats two thousand miles away, or a panel of judges from Harvard, should have anything to say about the Order of the Moose in Anytown, when the members of that order best know their needs and the needs of their community and how to address them according to their neighbors' sense of the common good.

But the more fundamental basis for the Principle of the Home is not utilitarian, but human: "To enter into a [free association] is the natural right of man; and the State is bound to protect natural rights, not to destroy them; and if it forbid its citizens to form associations, it contradicts the very principle of its own existence" (*RN*, 240).

Reclaiming Catholic Social Teaching

Suppose — I'm dreaming wildly — that an arm of the government were to dictate to the Kiwanis Club that it must admit women as members. There are plenty of free associations for men and women both: the Salvation Army, Alcoholics Anonymous, Common Cause, and so forth. What's at issue is not whether there may be associations of that kind, but whether there may *not* be associations of the other kind. Pope Leo would find it appalling that any State should forbid men from coming together for the common good or dictate the terms of their union. We can say the same thing about the Boy Scouts. Should the government compel the Scouts to organize themselves as the archons on the bench determine? Should we live in tyranny? Should we deny the fundamental right of free association?

I dwell upon the Principle of the Home because it helps to clarify the wisdom of the first two principles and to show how they all work together. Laws cannot, alone, make people good. They do have an instructive value; they restrain vicious actions and may, much less reliably, foster virtuous actions. But the moral law requires a human face. It's in our human associations, and not by our subatomic status as citizens of a sprawling State, that we learn virtue. The State can address a few specific troubles, with middling effectiveness, and at great strain — disaster relief, for instance. Beyond that the State must not try to go, because the State *should not* usurp the roles of the family, the fraternity, and the town, even if the State *could* assume those roles effectively — which it *cannot do*: its arrogant attempts have wrought more harm than a hundred hurricanes ever could. The State's role is to observe the moral law, to promote by general laws the conditions wherein people of ordinary virtue and industry can thrive, providing assistance in extreme cases, and to restrain its ambitions, honoring the independence and the interdependence of human beings in families, parishes, churches, guilds, fraternities, sororities, and other unions created for mutual help and the common good.

All this implies the fourth principle, what I'll call the Principle of the Human Person. Man, made free, in the image of God, must not be subordinated to abstractions. We accept no fatalisms. We will not subsume human commerce under a law, whether Marxist or Benthamite, socialist or capitalistic, which "determines" what is good and bad. We obey God, not man.

It is not right for the strong man to squeeze concessions from his weaker brother. Mutual consent is insufficient. A desperate man may accept ten dollars a day to go down a coal mine, but he has no moral right to do so, nor does the owner of the mine have a moral right to suggest it. A desperate woman may offer her body for money, but she has no moral right to do so, nor does the bawd on the corner have the right to be her broker. We must remember what people are, what (and Whom) they are for.

Natural justice trumps consent: "Let it be taken for granted that workman and employer should, as a rule, make free agreements, and in particular should agree freely as to the wages; nevertheless, there underlies a dictate of natural justice more imperious and ancient than any bargain between man and man, namely, that remuneration ought to be sufficient to support a frugal and well-behaved wage earner" (*RN*, 236). Well-behaved: Leo's Latin reads *bene morato*, describing a man formed by good moral habits. It means a great deal more than that he shows up for work on time.

A Society of Societies

That just wage implies an intricate set of human interchanges. The worker and the employer must treat one another fairly; if the employer does not bow in homage to the labor market, the employee does not do as little as he can to preserve his job. The employer must find worthwhile and feasible work for the work-man to do—for he too must stay in business. The employee must use those wages wisely. They are meant for him in his capacity as a social being: for the family he is supporting or will someday support. "If he be a sensible man," says the Pope, he will not find it hard "to study economy; and he will not fail, by cutting down expenses, to put by some little savings and thus secure a small income. Nature and reason alike would urge him to do this" (*RN*, 237).

Leo's ideal is not State control, with individuals as wardens, but a society built up of societies; a culture truly *social*, based on human friendships and family ties and alliances. "The law," he says, "should favor ownership, and its policy should be to induce as many as possible of the humbler class to become owners." Again, we must resist the tendency to abstraction. It will not do for the State to seize all property and parcel it out again accord-ing to some mathematical formula. The virtue of ownership is akin to the virtue of the family, of the self-governing town, of the free association. It arouses a love the State cannot command: "Men always work harder and more readily when they work on what belongs to them; nay, they learn to love the very soil that yields, in response to the labor of their hands, not only food to eat but an abundance of good things for themselves and for those that are dear to them" (*RN*, 237-38).

William Bradford, longtime leader of the Plymouth Colony, saw the principle at work. When the Pilgrims first settled in Plymouth, since they were members of a joint stock company, financed by stockholders in England, and shared by contract the proceeds of the company, they at first organized their labor accordingly. That is, there was no private property, and women cooked meals and washed clothes for the men in general rather than for their own husbands and children. That produced a lot of hard feelings, especially from those who believed that they were doing more for the general good than others were; and the common land was largely neglected, because no one had particular responsibility for it. At that, Bradford and the members of the compact returned to common sense and private ownership of houses, barns, and gardens, regardless, said Bradford, of philosophers (he has Plato in mind) who dream up republics that have never existed and never will.

We Americans allow trade unions. We protect workers from various forms of abuse. Those battles were fought and won long before I was born. What we've done lately, though, in the so-called social issues, is to violate every single tenet of Catholic social teaching as proclaimed by Pope Leo XIII.

One of the most noticeable things about *Rerum novarum* is that Leo does not launch into a series of recommendations regarding the working classes. He does not begin with politics and national economics; he does not build upon sand. He begins with a metaphysical meditation on what man is—so he turns, not to the State, but to that foundational society. "Hence," he says, thinking of God's first command to Adam and Eve, to be fruitful and multiply, "we have the family; the society of a man's house—a society limited indeed in numbers, but no less a true society, anterior to every kind of State or nation, invested with rights and duties of its own, totally *independent* of the civil community" (*RN*, 214; emphasis mine).

What does he mean by that word *independent*? Do families owe nothing to the community? May they break laws at will? Not at all. We conceive of independence as the ruthless autonomy of the individual will. Pope Leo is using the word in a different and more radical sense. The family does not *hang from* the civil community. It is not the community that defines the family, but the family that constitutes the community. We are talking here about an order of being. The family is anterior to every kind of State, not temporally, although that is certainly true, but in *being*. Families are not justified by the good they bring to the State; the State is justified by the good it brings to families. The State can bring good to families, though, only if it recognizes their anterior status, and their legitimate sphere of authority.

Catholic social teaching condemns the statist usurpation of the family, whether that usurpation is openly hostile or is cloaked in beneficence. Extreme necessities should be met by public aid, and gravely criminal actions by a member of the family against the family must be punished. "This is not to deprive citizens of their rights," says Leo, "but justly and properly to safeguard and preserve them. But the rulers of the State must go no further: here nature bids them stop. Paternal authority can be neither abolished nor absorbed by the State; for it has the same source as human life itself" (*RN*, 215).

Thus far and no further. But we now have States that allow free license to all vices lethal to the family. Pope Leo would have understood that demonic strategy.

He still believed, however, that honest statesmen would see the harm. Here, in his letter to the archbishop of Verona (February 8, 1893), he notes that contemporary States had absorbed into themselves all the rights of families (notice that they come first in the Pope's mind) and of individuals, on the grounds of providing for the common weal. But to a State that dismisses every divine and Christian law, it means nothing "if sins should multiply, either by seeking out illicit [sexual] unions, or persevering in them; even though reason, faith, and history should bring forth evidence that corruption in morals cuts a society's sinews, spoils it, consumes it" (translation mine; 1132).

Leo could not have foreseen, however, that "the State" would become an interest in its own right, a new aristocracy, but utterly detached from locale and tradition and unknown to their subjects. A nation thrives by moral rule. But the State, the cancerous Metastate, thrives for a while by immorality. It helps to cause the chaos it then pretends to ameliorate. Strong and self-reliant families hurt the Metastate, so the Metastate rewards profligacy and licentiousness and promotes the easy severance of father from children. The Metastate knows that if people but make an earnest attempt to govern themselves by the Ten Commandments and the gospel, they will be free and prosperous, and the Metastate will shrivel. Perish the thought.

Small Platoons

If we think of the State as the land where we were born, we will more easily turn from abstractions to a full-blooded reality. I cannot feel real loyalty to a place that may well be half a world away from me. That is why the nation, for its own health, should encourage such loyalties. That is, it is in the interest of the nation that people should feel loyalty to what Edmund Burke happily called the "small platoons" into which they are born, the places, the people, their families stretching back far into the past, their music, their schools, their marriages, their food and drink, their worship and prayer.

That is why, if we want to help the workingman, we should turn first to the people nearest to him. We have seen that Pope Leo XIII defends the right of a workingman to receive wages sufficient to support his family, in a becoming manner, if he but practices the virtues of diligence and frugality in an ordinary way. He says that our hearts and our very entrails must be moved with compassion for those who earn their bread by the sweat of their brow (*Il y a deux ans* [October 20, 1889], 985).

We have also seen that the Pope defends the right of laborers to form free associations to secure just wages and humane working conditions. In particular, the *guilds* are close to Leo's heart, sodalities that provided for both the material and spiritual welfare of their members and their families. We have seen him insist that the family is anterior to the State and possesses authority, rights, and duties to which the State must defer.

As to the individual, he possesses a right to ownership that the State cannot abrogate by excessive taxation, but he does *not* have the moral right to do with his wealth what he pleases, since God has granted him that wealth so that *he may put it to use* to benefit those less fortunate than he.

Above all, Pope Leo reminds us that without the virtue of religion, the State becomes little more than a compact of selfishness and sensuality, not worthy of human allegiance. As to poverty and rapacity, "religion alone," says the Pope, "can avail to destroy the evil at its root," so that "all men should rest persuaded that the main thing needful is to return to real Christianity, apart from which all the plans and devices of the wisest will prove of little avail" (*RN*, 247).

Now it's time to put these principles together.

Let us turn again to the guilds. These were associations of craftsmen in the Middle Ages, centered in towns. They trained boys in manual labor that required much skill: there were guilds for shoemakers, carpenters, weavers, blacksmiths, silversmiths, milliners, masons, glaziers, and so forth. The university, in fact, began as a student and faculty union, a guild for scholars. The guilds did what Leo advises Catholic unions to do, "to arrange for a continuous supply of work at all times and seasons, as well as to create a fund out of which the members may be effectually helped in their needs, not only in cases of accident but also in sickness, old age, and distress" (*RN*, 245). In other words, they were *insurance organizations* in several senses. They insured instruction for the young. They insured employment for the men, with a steady income. They insured their members against trouble and provided for widows and orphans.

They also insured food for the journey. "What advantage can it be to a workingman," asks Leo, "to obtain by means of a society all that he requires, and to endanger his soul for lack of spiritual food?" (*RN*, 244). The old guilds, then, celebrated their patronal feasts and took part in the local religious holidays; the new Catholic sodalities of Leo's time practiced communal prayer and reception of the sacraments. "Religious instruction," says Leo, should enjoy the foremost place in the life of these associations: "Let the workingman be urged and led to the worship of God, to the earnest practice of religion, and, among other things, to the keeping holy of Sundays and holydays." That was not just for the sake of civic order, for Leo, near the end of his life, wrote that he had always sought to "elevate the minds of men to the goods of the world beyond," and to subject their "earthly life"—his Italian word is *pellegrinaggio*, pilgrimage—"to the heavenly one" (*PAA*, 568). What a fine thing that would be, to be one with others in your trade, praying together, and strengthening one another on the pilgrimage.

How far is such a guild from the National Education Association or the American Federation of State, County, and Municipal Employees? As far as the heavens are above the earth, or the mountains above the sea.

Reclaiming Catholic Social Teaching

"But are guilds practical?" asks the skeptic, forgetting the lessons of Jesus, who reminds us that if we seek heaven and God's righteousness first, we need not worry about what we will eat or drink or wear, because we will be given earth into the bargain. Let me assert what is *not* practical. It's *not* practical to discourage the formation of families by spending $45,000 a year per broken or never-quite-built household, with the result that millions of children grow up without a father in the home. It's *not* practical to burn $10,000 a year per child in schools whose students live in moral chaos, schools where youths are taught neither good books nor the fine arts nor any remunerable trade.

All human relations bring morality into play. All rights come bound with duties. It isn't that the duties counterbalance the rights, but that truly human exchanges are gifts of the self, and a gift calls for a gift in exchange, if but the gift of a grateful heart. Let us stipulate that the employer should give the workman a living wage. Why? The wise father in *How Green Was My Valley*, as I've remarked, has given us the fundamental reason: "Because they are men, as we are." But this implies that the workingman will do for the employer something worth the living wage. This is where guilds come in. I must not expect somebody to give my son a living wage to cut crescent moons in the doors of outhouses. My son must be trained to provide for his employer benefits or products that call for that living wage. Who will train him? That's the responsibility of the men in the Catholic societies.

Note here that employer, employee, guildsman, and apprentice are all called upon to act in their truly *human* interest, and not merely for immediate monetary gain. The wealthy man has a right to his property, but a responsibility to see that his property provides for others; this responsibility he may best fulfill not by bowing to a confiscatory State, but by *employing* other people.

The State

The employee has a right to a living wage, and a responsibility to earn it by doing *good work*, work of intrinsic value. The guildsman and his fellows act, justly, to dampen the fluctuations in available work, and to ensure standards of excellence, but they must also labor to train the young in their trades, even if that means adding to the number of tradesmen nearby. The apprentice, too young yet to have a family, will accept lower pay now in exchange for instruction and will obey his teachers, while demanding his *human* right to be taught well. Michelangelo himself was the product of such a system.

Here someone objects, "But the *market* must determine who enters what line of work, and what the remuneration will be." Yes, but the *market* is not some Being set above us. It is an abstraction to denote the generality of human decisions. We are not discussing what to do, given a *market* and its symbiotic State that encourage waste, stupidity, and vice. We don't want that market and that State. We want a different culture altogether—or I should say, we want a *culture*, as opposed to mass education, mass politics, and mass entertainment. And this is something that the National Education Association and its like are impotent to bring about.

Take a look at the devastated city of Detroit, where neighborhoods are being plowed under and returned to grassland. Are there no workmen to repair the rotting houses? Nobody to drain the swampy alleys? No plumbers to lay new pipes? No masons to shore up the walls?

Well, no, there aren't—but where have they gone? Look at the works of extraordinary beauty that tradesmen used to create, such as New York's Grand Central Station, or the national buildings on Independence Mall. Why are our public buildings now so drab and cheap?

The thing is, there is not some independent quantity of work "out there," floating freely. We can change what we want; and sometimes work breeds more work, as when people turn to a work of beauty and say, "We would like that in our town too."

We see, then, that for Pope Leo all these moral principles belong together. We can't talk about a living wage without talking about laboring families, nor about laboring families without talking about fathers, nor about fathers without talking about youths, nor about youths or anybody else without talking about instruction, both for earthly and for spiritual gain. What do we in America now do? We have unions that are entirely worldly and that do virtually no training of youth; a welfare system that punishes the unwed mother when she marries; a tax system that confiscates property so as to foster dependency among the poor and the growth of the State; an educational system that views children as wards of the State and parents as guardians under State sufferance; a judicial system morbidly suspicious of religion, the only thing that ever gives substance to a culture or a society in the first place; and the worst kind of poverty of all, spiritual destitution, afflicting rich and poor alike, so that the poor are often no closer to God than the rich are, being merely less successful in their selfishness. And we think we are too wise to listen to an old man in Rome.

Conclusion

A Catholic Order

*One thing have I desired of the Lord, that will
I seek after; that I may dwell in the house of the
Lord all the days of my life, to behold the beauty
of the Lord, and to inquire in his temple.*
—Psalm 26:4

*Go ye therefore, and teach all nations,
baptizing them in the name of the Father,
and of the Son, and of the Holy Ghost:
teaching them to observe all things whatsoever
I have commanded you: and lo, I am with you
always, even unto the end of the world. Amen.*
—Matthew 28:19-20

My earliest memory of church comes from when I was a little boy, and my mother took me with her to daily Mass at noontime. She went sometimes, walking the half mile down the hill to our church in the river valley below.

I don't remember seeing the priest. I was too small to peer above the pews and the altar rail. It seemed to me that his voice was coming from the corner of the ceiling and the wall. What I do remember, and what is still in that church now, were the people of a great and holy and mysterious society.

Some of them were painted in the spaces between the stained glass windows and had their names memorialized below them. I had taught myself to read while I was still three years old, so I became familiar with them, even before I knew who they really were. There was a red-bearded King David with a harp. There was King Solomon, with what looked like ears of grain in his halo; I had no idea why. There was Moses with his staff and silver rays that seemed to strike his forehead. There was the priest Esdras, as we knew him in those days, reading from a long scroll. There was a young Gideon, blowing his trumpet.

People, people everywhere, doing things I didn't yet understand: Thomas More denying the request of a clearly unhappy King Henry VIII; Ignatius of Loyola, begging Francis Xavier to join him in his quest; Patrick preaching to the Irish; our Lady appearing to the children at Fátima; our Lady giving the rosary to Dominic, while Thomas Aquinas and Catherine of Siena look on in adoration; a crowd of saints everywhere, from Italy, from Ireland, from Palestine, from America, from two thousand years ago, from the Middle Ages, from just the other day; men and women, mothers and fathers, children, priests, nuns, Michael with his sword, Pope Pius X raising the Host for a kneeling girl and boy. You could not look at anything blank or lonely or merely functional in that church.

I was a shy child, but there I felt at home. It was many, many years before I would feel comfortable at, say, a large party, or in some big public space for general use. Such places are for social games, some of them harmless and pleasant, some of them cold and ruthless; and often what you find there, beneath all the chat, is but the vague specter of a society, friends who are not really friends, and the irresistible sense that everyone wants very much to belong, but no one does, because there is nothing substantial for them to belong to.

What a Catholic Society Can Never Be

I have tried to understand, as a whole, the social thinking of Pope Leo XIII. It is surely beyond my capacity. What I have understood, I'd like now to present in summary.

I shall begin with what a Catholic society can never be.

Jesus tells us that a house divided against itself cannot stand. A Catholic society cannot be divided against itself. It holds with our mother and teacher, as Pope John XXIII put it. It holds with the Church.

Jesus tells us that it would be better for a man to have a great millstone hung around his neck and to be thrown into the sea than for any one of the "little ones" to be scandalized. A Catholic society will not tolerate the seduction and corruption of children. It will not tolerate holding children hostage to the caprices or the sexual wants of adults—of fornicators, adulterers, pornographers, or sodomites. It will not establish schools as training grounds for the faithless and squalid. It will not sentence to death unwanted children.

Jesus tells us that God is the author of marriage. A Catholic society cannot settle for compromise in the matter of divorce. Jesus tells us that man may not put asunder what God has joined.

Jesus tells us that it is as hard for a rich man to enter the kingdom of heaven as it is for a camel to pass through the eye of a needle. A Catholic society must always remain wary of worldly prosperity. Riches may be a blessing—may be—but whether they are or not, they carry a grave duty. The love of money is the root of all evil.

Jesus tells us that whatever we do to the least among us, we do to Him. We cannot foist our duties upon others. We must feed the hungry, clothe the naked, house the homeless, tend the sick, visit the prisoners, bury the dead, and assist the widow and orphan. We must do this. It is a personal responsibility.

Jesus tells us that the clean of heart are blessed and that they will see God. We cannot then live like swine. We cannot shrug at filth, no matter that it may come from people who do not believe. We cannot make light of the high virtue of purity.

Jesus shows us by example that the kingdoms of this world, in a mysterious sense, are in the gift of the prince of darkness. He does not mean that we should not love our country. He Himself loved the lost sheep of Israel. But a Catholic people loves their country best by loving God first. If they cannot serve in political office, as they could not in the days before Constantine, they must remember the case of Pontius Pilate. A little water does not wash away the blood of the innocent.

Jesus tells us that He alone is the bread of life, that He alone has living water to give. He is the Good Shepherd; if we have Him, there is nothing we shall want. We do not look for shepherds elsewhere. We do not bow down to political ideologies or systems. We do not expect salvation from presentiments of the great new earth to come. We do not worship the supposedly inevitable march of history. We do not worship an emperor, whatever his name may be.

Jesus tells us that the Son of Man has nowhere to lay His head. He tells us that He is in the world, but not of the world. And we too must labor in the world and not be of the world, loving the world best when we have our hearts set upon the Creator and the Redeemer of the world.

What a Catholic Order May Be

I see a land of sinners. All lands are so.

But there is something different about these sinners. It is hard to explain. I see it in the grave countenances of the altar boys as they look to the elevation of the Host. I see it in the merry eyes of the old people as they drink beer at the parish hall and talk about something wild they did long ago.

There is no word for "lonely" in Middle English, probably because people were too near to one another and had to depend upon one another for common human things — such as making music, or doing the washing, or butchering a pig, or mourning a child, or building a church. Whatever the material conditions of life may be, I see a *human* life.

It's not a life of prigs and prudes. Genuine purity shines out like the glow of the sun on the green grass; it makes everything look fresher, younger, sweeter, more alive. Children are everywhere. Some of the children toddle about on two legs and a cane.

A Catholic Order

Most of the children—I'll use Shakespeare's words—are like
lambs that frisk in the sun, and bleat the one at the other. No
one needs background music at work; children are that music.

Unless you become as little children, says the Lord, you shall
not enter into the kingdom of heaven. I see a land where people
protect innocence—not ignorance, but innocence—as a tender
and lovely flower. Boys and girls like one another, then can't
stand one another, and bicker and quarrel, and kiss, and marry
so that they can bicker and quarrel more conveniently, and kiss,
and do the blessed thing that makes for more boys and girls in
the world. Everything they are taught about their own sex and
the other is aimed at that end, and even with men and women
as imperfect as we are, that is as right as rain. So there are dances,
dances all the time, and song. And little children learn to dance,
with the old people taking part or watching, and lads and lasses
in the bloom of youth, flushed with happiness, or wistful longing,
or the pangs of love, or sheer innocent mirth.

I see schools. Who are the teachers? They too are children.
Many of them are women dressed in habits. When their hair is
covered, all you can see is the face—the expressive lips, the eyes.
They have given their lives, their youth, their talent, to teach
the children. People treat them with courtesy and deference.
They call themselves sisters, but they are mothers, all of them.
They have curious names, like Perpetua, Agatha, and Felicity.
Their devotion is contagious. They believe they have the best of
spouses, Christ Himself. They would no sooner expose children
to moral filth than they would expose them to typhus or malaria.
Even the saltiest men at the public house watch their language
when their little sisters, their superiors, pass by.

Those schools—what do the children study there? Everything worthwhile, and all in the light of Christ. Pope Leo said

it better than I can: "It is needful then not simply to instruct children in religion for certain hours of the day, but everything else about the school should be fragrant with the sense of Christian piety" (ME, 1322; translation mine).

I see people with people. Not many are rich, and everybody has enough, because everybody has a family that is intact, and everybody has neighbors. I see a baseball club, a shooting club, weekly card tournaments at the Knights of Columbus, a women's Welcoming Committee, a school board overseeing the Catholic school, three troops of Boy Scouts, three troops of Girl Scouts, a band practicing their music out of the clarinet player's garage, a union for the local barbers, a union for the local electricians, a union for the local carpenters, a cemetery committee, three or four civic beneficent societies, a local theater troupe, and a policemen's benevolent society. I see ordinary human life, if wise and restrained laws, and wiser and self-restraining virtues, give it room to flourish.

And it is ordinary: it is in order, and it is or was eminently possible.

Our Source of Unity

How do we build such a society? That is the wrong question. We do not build it at all. We allow Christ to build it for us. The source of our union does not lie in our will, our cleverness, our political machinery, even our virtues, such as they are. It lies in Christ.

Recall the disciples after Pentecost, who, "continuing daily with one accord in the temple, and breaking bread from house to house, did eat their meat with gladness and singleness of heart, praising God, and having favour with all the people" (Acts 2:46-47). It was not their bringing people to the Church that made them glad. It was their gladness that brought people to the Church, and their gladness came solely from the risen Christ, their Redeemer. What Pope Leo recommends to priests applies to all the faithful: "Frequent meditation upon the things of heaven wonderfully nourishes and strengthens [evangelical] virtue, and makes it always ready and fearless of the greatest difficulties for the good of others," for they will see "how sad it is that so many men, redeemed by Jesus Christ, should run headlong to eternal ruin; and by meditation upon the divine nature they will themselves be more strongly moved, and will more effectually excite others to the love of God" (*EIA*, 176). Where love for Christ grows cool, so will love for man.

So I now come to the heart of the Church's social teaching, as Pope Leo shows us. It is the Most Holy Eucharist. Hence his encyclical *Mirae caritatis* (1902), written near the very end of his long pontificate.

It too is a *social* encyclical; it is the most socially significant of them all. "Our lot has been cast in an age that is bitterly hostile to justice and truth," he says (MC, 517). Men of talents, instead of elevating their brothers, urge them on instead to "the race for wealth, to a struggle for the possession of commodities which minister to the love of comfort and display," and as a result, "human society," alienated from God, "instead of enjoying that peace in its possessions for which it had sought, is shaken and tossed like one who is in the agony and heat of fever" (MC, 522). "Men have forgotten that they are children of God and brethren of Jesus Christ; they care for nothing except their own individual interests; the interests and the rights of others they not only make light of, but often attack and invade" (MC, 527). That selfishness is of a piece with their contumacy against God: "Nor is there any motive by which many are hurried on with more passionate fury, than the desire utterly to banish God not only from the civil government, but from every form of human society" (MC, 533).

When Jesus first revealed to His followers that He would Himself be the bread from heaven, an earnest of eternal blessings to all who partake thereof, many of them walked away. "This is an hard saying," they grumbled. "Who can hear it?" (John 6:60). Yet that promise was not meant simply for them as individuals. "The bread that I will give," says Jesus, "is my flesh, which I will give for the life of the world" (John 6:51). Many Catholics will now easily accept the doctrine of the Eucharist as it applies to them, or as it applies to Catholics as a group, but not see that Jesus means exactly what He says here. Pope Leo points it out. The Eucharist is *for the life of the world*. And Christ declared Himself to be *the life*: "I am the way, the truth, and the life" (John 14:6).

For Leo, that does not simply mean that those who receive the Eucharist in a devout and reverent manner will be directed toward the things of heaven rather than the things of earth. Recall his constant affirmation of the full presence of the Creator in the creation He loves. "Away then," he cries, "with the widespread but most mischievous error of those who give it as their opinion that the reception of the Eucharist is in a manner reserved for those narrow-minded persons (as they are deemed) who rid themselves of the cares of the world in order to find rest in some kind of professedly religious life" (MC, 521-522). The Eucharist is Christ present among men, here and now, as in heaven. Therefore, just as Jesus had fed the multitudes at the Sea of Tiberias with loaves and fishes, so too does His presence among us feed us in the world we live in, and it has the power to transform that world utterly. Here Pope Leo appeals to plain historical fact, in a passage that I have cited already but which bears repeating: "No sooner had *the goodness and kindness of God our Savior appeared* than there at once burst forth a certain creative force which issued in a new order of things and pulsed through all veins of society, civil and domestic," giving rise to new human relations, "new rights and new duties, public and private," a new direction "to government, to education, to the arts," and, "most important of all, man's thoughts and energies were turned towards religious truth and the pursuit of holiness. Thus was life communicated to man, a life truly heavenly and divine" (MC, 520).

A sincere devotion to the Blessed Sacrament, Leo says, will bring unity among men again by fostering three virtues: faith, patience, and charity.

Faith is the heart of this new inner life and this new way of living among men. In these days it is of most urgent need, because while in former days heretics attacked particular articles of the Faith, it now "has come to this, that men deny altogether that there is anything above and beyond nature" (MC, 523). But "nothing can be better adapted to promote a renewal of the strength and fervor of faith in the human mind than the mystery of the Eucharist." When a child sees, as I have seen, a man of the most powerful scientific intellect kneel in adoration before the Lord, present in the tabernacle, with the flame in the red sanctuary lamp flickering, it is as Leo says, "the mind finds its nourishment the objections of rationalists are brought to naught, and abundant light is thrown on the supernatural order" (MC, 524). If earthly nature is all there is, then this world is a wilderness, and only greater cunning separates man from beast. But "the earth is the LORD'S, and the fullness thereof; the world, and they that dwell therein" (Psalm 24:1). He, the

Lord of nature, in the miracle of the Eucharist, suspends the laws of that nature and has confirmed that miracle by "prodigies wrought in His honor, both in ancient times and in our own, of which in more than one place there exist public and notable records and memorials."

Then the Eucharist recommends patience to us — the virtue that the worldly will not endure, because when their dreams of ambition or glory or wealth are dashed, they have no one and nothing left for their hope. But those who adore and receive the Eucharist have implanted within their frail bodies "a principle of resurrection, a seed of immortality" (MC, 526). Yet that seed bears fruit only in its being broken, as was Christ upon the Cross. For the Eucharist is a memorial of His Passion and death and proclaims to the Christian "the necessity of a salutary self-chastisement." It is a sacrifice and therefore "a standing exhortation to all manner of toil, and a solemn and severe rebuke to those carnal pleasures which some are not ashamed so highly to praise and extol."

And the Eucharist brings charity, as it is itself the supreme gift of God to man: the very life of Christ, body and blood, soul and divinity. Because men have forgotten that they are children of God and brothers in Jesus Christ, we find "arrogance, oppression, fraud on the part of the more powerful: misery, envy, and turbulence among the poor" (MC, 527). What remedy can man concoct for those spiritual evils? No human laws will do, says the Pope. We need instead the fruit of the Sacrament, "the true spirit of Jesus Christ and a genuine charity."

It is not just a feeling. It is a real, spiritual, and manifest experience of unity. Leo cites Aquinas and Augustine in comparing the material components of the Host to the people who worthily receive it: "Our Lord has bequeathed to us His body and blood under the form of substances in which a multitude of things have been reduced to unity, for one of them, namely bread, consisting as it does of many grains is yet one, and the other, that is to say wine, has its unity of being from the confluent juice of many grapes; and therefore St. Augustine elsewhere says: 'O Sacrament of mercy, O sign of unity, O bond of charity!'" (MC, 528; cf. *Summa Theologica* III, Q. 79, art. 1). See, kneeling at the altar, praying silently and awaiting the approach of the priest as he moves from communicant to communicant, one by one, the small boy whose chin barely clears the rail, his many-wrinkled grandfather beside him, a young mother holding an infant in her arms, the schoolteacher, the professor of English, the man who spends his days putting roofs on houses, the lanky youth, the beautiful girl, the poor man, the rich man, all gathered at the table, in the only place on earth these days where they will all so gather, "all sharing alike in this heavenly banquet" (MC, 529).

And they are not the only ones present, either. That is because they belong to a sweet society far transcending any society upon earth, one whose capital is not built with marble, whose boundaries admit everyone who longs to enter, whose wealth is not counted in gold, and whose laws are not the objects of clever men. Those who have gone before us in the Faith are present too, "for the communion of saints, as every one knows, is nothing but the mutual communication of help, expiation, prayers, blessings, among all the faithful, who, whether they have already attained to the heavenly country, or are detained in the purgatorial fire, or are yet exiles here on earth, all enjoy the common franchise of that city whereof Christ is the head, and the constitution is charity" (MC, 529-530). *That* is a franchise to march arm in arm for! *That* is the constitution that never fails!

Reclaiming Catholic Social Teaching

The Eucharist is not the *expression of our human love*. It is the expression of Christ's *divine love* and the cause of divine love within us. Therefore, says Leo, the Church "strives to promote the veneration of this august mystery by surrounding it with holy ceremonies" (MC, 531). It is not to be shelved in a back room. It is not to be treated as if it were a pleasant diversion. The Eucharist "is to be regarded as the center towards which the spiritual life of a Christian in all its ambit gravitates; for all other forms of devotion, whatsoever they may be, lead up to it, and in it find their point of rest" (MC, 530).

Therefore Pope Leo, encouraging frequent and reverent reception of the Sacrament, urges Catholics also to unite in special bonds for its veneration. "Worthy of special mention," he says, "are the Confraternities instituted either with the object of carrying out the Eucharistic ritual with greater splendor" — not, note well, with indifference, or worldly plainness — "or for the perpetual adoration of the venerable Sacrament by day and night" (MC, 534), along with other liturgical actions that may have fallen into disuse, such as "intercessory prayers before the Blessed Sacrament exposed for the veneration of the faithful, solemn processions, devout visits to God's tabernacle, and other holy and salutary practices of the same kind; nothing must be omitted which a prudent piety may suggest as suitable" (MC, 535).

I know where a truly Catholic social order is to be found. It is in a church full to bursting with sinners who know they are sinners and who know they have been redeemed; in a church whose faithful are too busy honoring God to take pride in themselves; in a church full of children, where the older ones take care of the younger ones; in a church full of people who rejoice when their fellows say to them, "Let us go up to the house of the Lord" (cf. Ps. 122:1); in a church that presses forward to the throne of God, whose elders fall down before Him who sits upon the throne, and worship Him who lives forever, and cast their crowns before the throne and cry, "You are worthy, O Lord, to receive glory and honor and power, for you have created all things, and for your pleasure they are and were created" (cf. Rev. 4:11).

Works Cited

Citations of the works of Pope Leo are as listed below. Numbers given in references refer to the page numbers in these volumes.

English translations from *The Great Encyclical Letters of Pope Leo XIII, Translations from Approved Sources* (New York, Cincinnati, Chicago: Benziger Brothers, 1903):

Aeterni Patris (AP), on the study of scholastic philosophy (August 4, 1879)

Arcanum divinae (AD), on Christian marriage (February 10, 1880)

Au Milieu des consolations (AMC), letter to the archbishop of Paris (December 23, 1900)

Au Milieu des solicitudes (AMS), letter to the bishops and faithful of France (February 16, 1892)

Exeunte iam anno (EIA), on the right ordering of Christian life (December 25, 1888)

Graves de communi (GDC), on Christian democracy (January 13, 1901)

Humanum genus (HG), on Freemasonry (April 20, 1884)

Reclaiming Catholic Social Teaching

Immortale Dei (*ID*), on the Christian constitution of states (November 1, 1885)

Inscrutabili (*I*), on the evils affecting modern society; their causes and remedies (April 21, 1878)

Libertas praestantissimum (*LP*), on human liberty (June 20, 1888)

Longinquae oceani (*LO*), on Catholicity in the United States (January 6, 1895)

Mirae caritatis (MC), on the Most Holy Eucharist (May 28, 1902)

Pervenuti all'anno (*PAA*), review of his pontificate (March 19, 1902)

Praeclara grationis publicae, on the reunion of Christendom (June 20, 1894)

Providentissimus Deus (*PD*), on the study of Holy Scripture (November 18, 1893)

Quod Apostolici muneris (*QAM*), on socialism, communism, nihilism (December 28, 1878)

Rerum novarum (*RN*), on the condition of the working classes (May 15, 1891)

Sapientiae Christianae (*SC*), on the chief duties of Christians as citizens (January 10, 1890)

Satis cognitum, on the unity of the Church (June 20, 1896)

Tametsi (*T*), on Christ our Redeemer (November 1, 1900)

Testem benevolentiae (*TB*), on true and false Americanism in religion (January 22, 1899)

Works Cited

English translations from Étienne Gilson, ed., *The Church Speaks to the Modern World: The Social Teachings of Leo XIII* (New York: Doubleday, 1954):

Diuturnum (D), on civil government (June 29, 1881)

In Plurimis, on slavery (letter to the bishops of Brazil, May 5, 1888)

English translation from Joseph Husslein, S.J., ed., *Social Wellsprings: Fourteen Epochal Documents by Pope Leo XIII* (Milwaukee: Bruce Publishing Company, 1940):

Laetitiae sanctae, on the Rosary and social questions (September 8, 1892)

All references to the original Latin, Italian, and French, and all citations of the following letters, are from Arthur F. Utz, ed., *La Doctrine Sociale De L'Eglise A Travers Les Siècles*, four vols. (Rome: Herder; Paris: Beauchesne et ses Fils, 1969):

Affari vos (AV), on the religious foundation of schools (letter to the bishops of Canada, December 8, 1897)

Cum multa sint (CMS), on religion and politics (December 8, 1882)

Il Divisamento di sancire, on civil marriage and religious marriage (letter to the archbishop of Verona, February 8, 1893)

Il y a Deux Ans, various responses for solving the labor question (December 20, 1889)

La Vostra lettera, on the Church hierarchy and the obedience of the faithful (letter to Cardinal Guibert, archbishop of Paris, June 17, 1885)

Les Evenements (*LE*), on the rights of the Church within the State (letter to the president of France, May 12, 1883)

Militantis Ecclesiae (*ME*), on an integrally Christian intellectual formation (August 1, 1897)

Officio sanctissimo, vindication of the Church, the perfect society, with regard to the State (letter to the bishops of Bavaria, December 22, 1887)

About the Author

Anthony Esolen is professor of English at Providence College. He is the author or translator of twelve books, including a three-volume translation of Dante's *Divine Comedy*; *Ironies of Faith: The Laughter at the Heart of Christian Literature*; and *The Beauty of the Word*, a running commentary on the new English translation of the Mass. He writes regularly for *Touchstone*, *Crisis*, *Public Discourse*, *Catholic World Report*, *First Things*, and *Magnificat*. He and his wife, Debra, and their children, Jessica and David, live in Rhode Island.

An Invitation

Reader, the book that you hold in your hands was published by Sophia Institute Press. Sophia Institute seeks to nurture the spiritual, moral, and cultural life of souls and to spread the Gospel of Christ in conformity with the authentic teachings of the Roman Catholic Church.

Our press fulfills this mission by offering translations, reprints, and new publications that afford readers a rich source of the enduring wisdom of mankind.

We also operate two popular online Catholic resources: CrisisMagazine.com and CatholicExchange.com.

Crisis Magazine provides insightful cultural analysis that arms readers with the arguments necessary for navigating the ideological and theological minefields of the day. *Catholic Exchange* provides world news from a Catholic perspective as well as daily devotionals and articles that will help you to grow in holiness and live a life consistent with the teachings of the Church.

In 2013, Sophia Institute launched Sophia Institute for Teachers to renew and rebuild Catholic culture through service to Catholic education. With the goal of nurturing the spiritual, moral, and cultural life of souls, and an abiding respect for the role and work of teachers, we strive to provide materials and programs that are at once enlightening to the mind and ennobling to the heart; faithful and complete, as well as useful and practical.

www.SophiaInstitute.com
www.CatholicExchange.com
www.CrisisMagazine.com
www.SophiaInstituteforTeachers.org